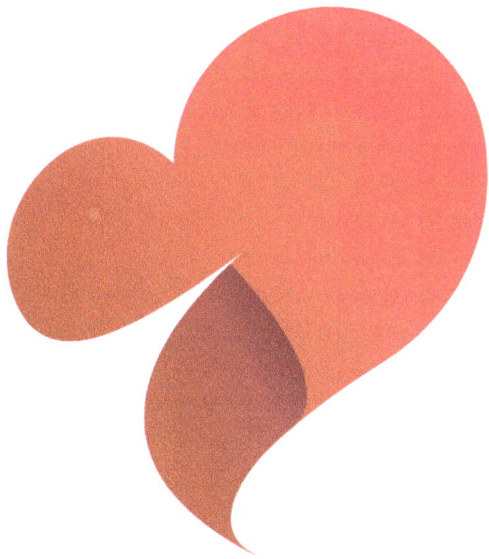

THE *Porsha* PRINCIPLES

A Practical Guide for Creating and
Sustaining Your Lifelong Honeymoon

by

Porsha Jones, LMFT
Michael Wilkinson, CMF

Published by Leadership Strategies Publishing
Atlanta, Georgia

Substantial discounts on bulk quantities are available to corporations, governments, nonprofits, and other organizations. For details and discount information, contact PorshaPrinciples.com.

Publisher's Cataloging-in-Publication Data

ISBN: 978-0-9722458-9-0

Manufactured in the United States of America

THE *Porsha*
PRINCIPLES

www.PorshaPrinciples.com

Dedicated to Our Adult Children,

Danielle, Gabrielle, and Kyree

That This May Serve As a Guide for You in

Creating and Sustaining Your Own Lifelong Honeymoon

Table of Contents

Acknowledgements

No book is created without the help and support of some very special people.

First and foremost, we want to thank our content review team. To Brian Gallagher, we thank you for your strategic focus and keen insights into how to insert greater nuance within the material. To Dr. Eileen Dowse, thank you for keeping us grounded in the research and broader in our thinking. Thank you, Kiné Corder, our book is much improved through your recommendation to implement deeper dives. Thanks to Sheila Lloyd and Ted Pearson, we have a more inclusive work. Daryl Bible provided unique insights that have made the book more readable and relatable. And thanks to Sadique Caldwell and Eric Pearson for their encouragement and unwavering support.

We give thanks to Dario Ruff and our marketing team at Avenue180, Rich Stern and our technology team at ZJS Technology, and Jon Harrison, our editor.

Finally, we thank our Creator for providing the thoughts, the tools, and the motivation to put the ideas into a form for others to use.

Porsha and Michael

Preface

*(The preface is written by Michael and is his description
of the story of the creation of The Porsha Principles.)*

If your Creator wanted each of us to do a special work—and I believe our Creator indeed has a special work for each of us to perform—would He give each one of us a random set of skills, a random set of interests, and hope that one day we stumble on what He wants us to do?

Or would He give us the exact talents we needed to get the job done, give us an intense passion for the work, prepare us our entire lives to be that vessel, and then bring the resources together at the time and place needed?

I personally believe the latter, and if you are reading this, I bet you do too. The words above describe what happened in the creation of *The Porsha Principles*. Let me take you through it.

When Porsha and I first met, there was something in the way she smiled, and the way we laughed together, and the complete ease and flow of our conversation, that I could sense the specialness we had together. And indeed, two days after our second date, I realized she had completely captured my heart. Within three months, while on a trip together, I found myself kissing her and prophesizing aloud, "With this kiss, I thee wed." It was a complete slip, and a shock to me. I wanted to grab the words out of the air … but no such luck. Surprisingly, she did not run away! That day we made a commitment to one another and agreed not to share it with anyone because they would likely think, as we did, that it was way too early for all that!

Fast forward to when the coronavirus pandemic took hold. We found ourselves sheltered in place working from home with our individual offices on opposite ends of our condo. From time to time I would pass by her door and happen to overhear one side of a conversation she was having through her EarPods. I could visualize the couple at the other end of her virtual call hanging on her every word. And for good reason. The concepts, the ideas, and the strategies were clear, concise, and so doable. It just made sense that if they were willing to do the work, they couldn't but overcome the issues they were facing.

I remember saying to Porsha at one point:

> *Sweetheart, you are sharing such life-changing jewels with people. You might want to consider writing these things down so that they are documented, and you can easily and consistently share them with every couple you work with.*

Of course, this was the facilitator in me wanting to teach the masses, versus the therapist in Porsha who focuses on individuals. In the weeks and months that followed we began doing just that, documenting some of her thoughts and ideas. It didn't take long for us to conclude we were creating more than just a list of ideas. These were principles and strategies for couples to live by; these were tools that could help many people keep their love alive and their honeymoon going.

And with that, the Porsha Principles were born. The more we worked on the principles, the more they took on a life of their own. We began visualizing a book, and then free webinars, and then the video series, and then the one-day workshop and weekend retreat.

Though we didn't see it at the time, in hindsight it became clear to us.

We were combining the marriage therapy work that Porsha had been doing for over a decade as one of the top marriage therapists in the southeast with the thirty years of experience I had gained in creating the leading company in the U.S. in providing facilitation training programs and professional facilitators.

Once more, our Creator at work.

The collaboration itself represents a true testament to the Porsha Principles in action. There were many times when the flow of the material was effortless and building on each other's ideas resulted in very creative solutions. Our similarities allowed us to experience tremendous joy with each other in the process and deepen our intimacy by practicing the principles together.

There were also times we had to remember to "lift our partner," "manage the differences," and even "repair ruptures." One of the significant differences that we poorly managed initially was balancing working on this very exciting project with giving our beautiful relationship the time and energy it deserved. As you will learn, my "James" was fulfilled by the progress we were making, but Porsha's "Porshey" was starving for the quality time and affection that fulfilled her. We quickly corrected the imbalance by remembering how important it was to each of us that our partner be fulfilled, by listening to understand the real need, by identifying solutions that could work for both of us, and by following through on the action and then checking in to ensure reconnection. The re-energizing that can come from your partner making a commitment to your happiness and then following through is awesome. And when that happens over and over again, that's what a lifelong honeymoon is all about.

The Book

Following the overview chapter, the book is organized based on the eight *Porsha Principles*.

1: Let them know you ... not your representative.
2: Cultivate intimacy ... at deeper levels.
3: Lift your partner ... every day.
4: Manage the differences ... with care and communication.
5: Avoid the fire starters ... they can ignite a blaze.
6: Address conflict ... resolve disagreements.
7: Repair the ruptures ... they can ruin you.
8: Profess, protect, and prioritize the relationship ... with your thoughts, words, and actions.

Within the principles you will discover:

- **Key concepts** that provide a foundational understanding of the principle and how it plays out in relationships.
- **Proactive strategies** that help you and your partner establish a strong foundation and prevent issues before they occur.
- **Intervention strategies** to use when you encounter roadblocks, including specific steps to take and sample words to use.
- **Deeper dives** that provide questions to consider in better understanding yourself and potential root causes of your behaviors and feelings.
- **Personal insights** from our life together, both examples of when we have been successful in applying a principle and times when our application was, shall I say, less than stellar.
- **Principles in practice** that give you and your partner specific exercises to do to enhance your skills in applying the principles in your relationship.

The Porsha Principles is not a one-and-done process. To sustain a high-quality relationship of love and fulfillment requires ongoing care and communication. Therefore, the book ends with you and your partner creating your Couple's Action Plan, your agreement and roadmap for using the principles to create and sustain your lifelong honeymoon.

Please keep in mind, *The Porsha Principles* is NOT intended to be a replacement for couples therapy or individual therapy, as we mention several times throughout the book. We believe therapy is a powerful vehicle for change and we highly recommend couples seek out quality professional assistance as needed. Though we do not offer this service ourselves, our website includes information about trusted partners and other available resources.

A Note about the Writing:
- For ease of writing, we have written the book in a conversational style with Porsha speaking in the first person (e.g., "From my research and experience, I have found …").
- For ease of reading, we use the "singular they" to avoid the awkward "his/her" (e.g., "Your partner might find that they …").

Our Hope

We believe that *The Porsha Principles* will be a catalyst for helping many, many couples to move out of the relationship desert and get back on the path to creating and sustaining a fruitful and rewarding lifelong honeymoon. We believe our Creator wants all His children to have relationships that truly reflect His love. We are here to help. And you can help too. If you find *The Porsha Principles* valuable, please spread the word. Share your experience with those in your network. Let them know of your experience and the value they can gain by finding ways to create and sustain their own lifelong honeymoon.

Michael

THE Porsha PRINCIPLES

A Practical Guide for Creating and
Sustaining Your Lifelong Honeymoon

by

Porsha Jones, LMFT
Michael Wilkinson, CMF

Overview

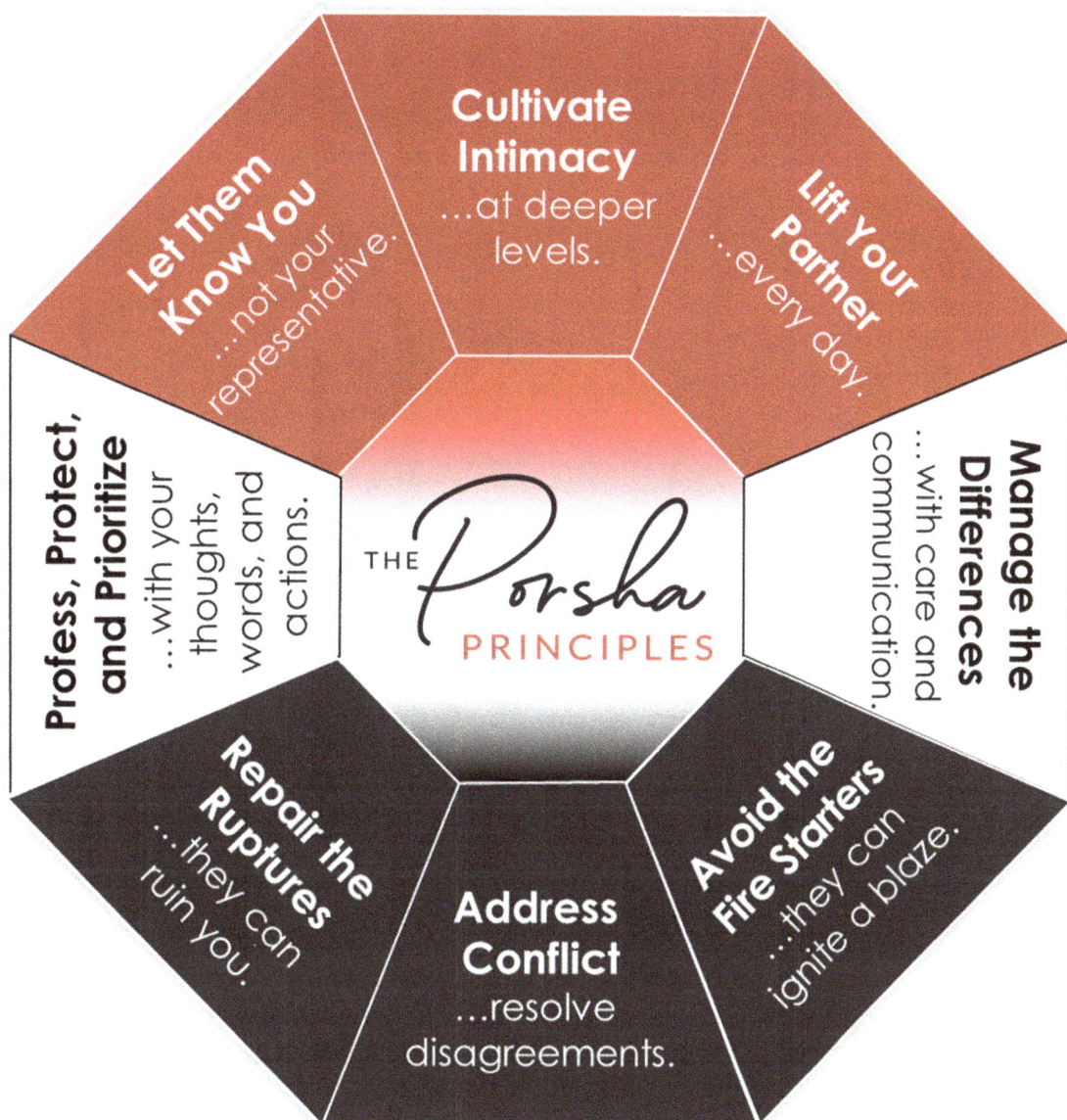

The Porsha PRINCIPLES

Cultivate Intimacy ...at deeper levels.

Let Them Know You ...not your representative.

Lift Your Partner ...every day.

Profess, Protect, and Prioritize ...with your thoughts, words, and actions.

Manage the Differences ...with care and communication.

Repair the Ruptures ...they can ruin you.

Address Conflict ...resolve disagreements.

Avoid the Fire Starters ...they can ignite a blaze.

What You Will Learn	**Foundation** • What is a lifelong honeymoon? • What causes the honeymoon to end? • What are the Porsha Principles and where did they come from? **Action** • How to learn and use the Porsha Principles • The Principles Assessment

The purpose of the Porsha Principles is to provide couples with key strategies that, if applied consistently in their relationship, will provide the foundation for creating and sustaining a lifelong honeymoon of love, joy, passion, support, and satisfaction.

Introducing Pam and Marcus

Like many couples, when Pam and Marcus first met, there was instant chemistry.

- In those early days of their relationship, Marcus frequently talked about how amazing she was. He had never met a woman who was so captivating. He loved just listening to her talk—he found that she always captured his attention with the way she described her day. When he would hear her laughter from across the room, it would warm his heart. He knew she was the best part of every day for him. He was in love.

- Pam was equally smitten. While in the past she had always chosen safe, stable men, Marcus was this and so much more. Though he was well educated and had an impressive job coaching executives, he was, without question, the sweetest man she had ever met. Despite his hectic schedule, he was always doing the things to let her know she was important to him. He was her Prince Charming. When people asked her about him, she found herself smiling. Her friends told her she seemed so much happier. They were right.

> **But fast forward five years and you would barely recognize them as the same couple.**

They were married after two years of dating and honeymooned in Hawaii. But fast forward five years and you would barely recognize them as the same couple.

- Pam's Prince Charming seems to have changed. While they used to spend so much time together, now she finds herself having to negotiate time for date nights, time for sex, time for him to do little projects around the house. He used to take pride and joy in supporting her. Now he just seems to dread it. What happened to that amazing man she married?

- When Marcus comes home at night and sees Pam's car in the driveway, his heart sinks; it used to give him a thrill. He knows he is going to walk into a house of complaints about what he hasn't done and how she deserves more. He is doing the best he can by working long hours to provide extra money to do the nicer things that they enjoy, and yet she doesn't appreciate the good that he is doing. She is constantly pointing out his faults. What happened to that amazing woman he married?

What Happened to the Honeymoon?

Why can't the honeymoon last forever? I think it can. My name is Porsha Jones; I am a licensed marriage and family therapist. While the story is fictional, it describes many of the couples that end up on my couch: two people who were once deeply in love find themselves in a place where the love seems to have dissipated.

Over my career I have been a catalyst to help hundreds of couples disrupt their dysfunction, repair serious ruptures, manage their differences, and create and sustain a new vision for their relationship so they can get back on the path to living—what I have come to call a **lifelong honeymoon**. It's real!

How do you do it? That's what the Porsha Principles are all about. These eight principles can be your catalyst for getting your relationship back to where you want it to be. Throughout this book I will use fictional couples and scenarios to introduce each of the principles and the related issues. I will then provide specific strategies to first prevent the issues from occurring, and second to address the issues if they are happening in your relationship.

Keep in mind that while the Porsha Principles can be a catalyst, you and your partner have to do the work. If you are ready, let's get started with what a lifelong honeymoon is and what causes it to end.

What Is a Lifelong Honeymoon?

> **A lifelong honeymoon is the experience of continual fulfilment and connection created by doing the things every day that let you and your partner know that they are affirmed, appreciated, and loved.**

Remember what it felt like when you and your partner went on your honeymoon? Remember the excitement you felt? The anticipation of having all this undivided one-on-one time to "deposit" so much love into one another? Remember the sense of joy and connection—feeling like you were the most important thing to your partner? The feeling of wanting this to last forever?

That's what a lifelong honeymoon is all about: living and relating with your partner in such a way that continually recreates, reinforces, and restimulates those same emotions over and over again—every day, every week, every month. It is living and connecting in a way that cultivates sustainable emotional safety and security.

A lifelong honeymoon is the experience of continual fulfilment and connection created by doing the things every day that let you and your partner know that they are affirmed, appreciated, and loved.

What Causes the Honeymoon to End?

I like thinking about a couple's relationship as being symbolized by a love pool. The "pool" is full, vibrant, and fun for the couple when the relationship is strong, when the pool is being constantly replenished, when both parties are pouring love into the pool through their acts of kindness, words of affirmation, spending time together, sharing common experiences, and so on. But when one party stops contributing and it triggers the other party to stop contributing as well, the pool can become stale and stagnant and can even begin to drain. And I suspect we have all seen couples where the love pool appears to be completely drained and partners can feel empty in the relationship. Not pretty.

For many couples the honeymoon phase lasts from six months to two years. And then what happens? People often say reality sets in: the pressures of careers, kids, in-laws, and other life stressors demand your time, drain your energy, and shift your focus off your partner. Partners start taking each other for granted. They stop thinking about their loved ones as the truly valuable and amazing person that they fell in love with. They stop contributing to the love pool and it begins to drain.

> **What causes the honeymoon to end? It's pretty simple really: People stop actively contributing to the love pool.**

Why does this happen? Scientific research[1] shows that the honeymoon period begins when a cascade of "in-love" hormones and neurotransmitters flood the brain as couples are in the very early stages of falling in love, creating those euphoric feelings. The honeymoon period ends when these hormones begin to die down, on average after two years.

So, what really causes the honeymoon to end? We stop doing the things that actively contribute to the love pool and continually restimulate those "in love" hormones.

In my practice I have found that many couples don't understand the concept of the love pool and the correlation to this research. And those who do understand the concept often see their partner's pool-draining behaviors only; they don't see their own. Then you layer on top of that:

- A couple's natural differences
- Poor communication skills
- Lack of willingness to be vulnerable
- Lack of conflict resolution strategies
- The inability to say they're sorry or that they made a mistake

And sometimes you have to wonder how these relationships could possibly have made it even two years! Fortunately, love is pretty durable, and relationships are often resilient; but instead of a lifelong honeymoon, love-draining behaviors can set a couple up for a lifelong struggle!

---

[1] Theresa Crenshaw, *The Alchemy of Love and Lust* (New York: Pocket Books, 1997).

A Summary of the Porsha Principles

From thousands of hours working with couples in varying levels of crisis, I have developed the Porsha Principles. Webster's defines a principle as *a comprehensive and fundamental law, doctrine, or assumption*. When I apply this definition to my work, I define the Porsha Principles as fundamental truths that serve as the foundation for successful relationships. These principles include key strategies that couples can use to create and sustain their lifelong honeymoon.

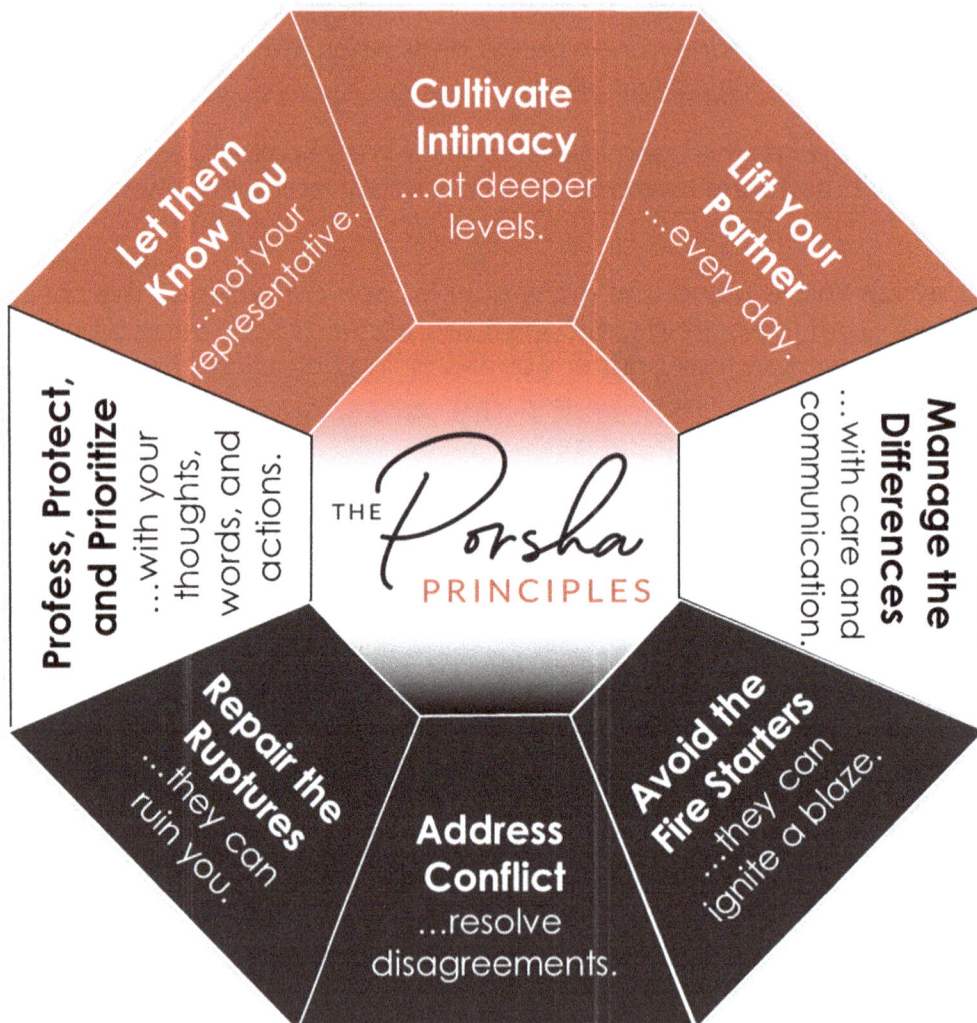

The eight *Porsha Principles* will guide you and your partner to having the kind of lifelong experiences that lead to hyper-fulfillment and highly sustained enjoyment of one another. The principles do three powerful things.

- The principles **provide proactive strategies** that help you and your partner learn to contribute to the love pool.
- They **raise your awareness** of behaviors that drain the love pool.
- They **provide intervention strategies** for times when repair to the pool is needed.

Let me give you a very quick overview of the eight principles.

Principle 1: Let them know you ... not your representative.

- You know how when you first meet someone, and they don't necessarily show you their real self?
- This can happen for many reasons. We all like to think that it's an attempt to put our best foot forward, to be liked or accepted. But often it's an attempt to hide our true self, our feelings, or even our current life situation.
- This inauthentic representative of one's self can show up regardless of whether you are in a short-term or long-term relationship.
- In this principle we talk about why this happens, how to spot the representative, and how to peel back the layers—both yours and your partner's—to reveal your authentic self.

Principle 2: Cultivate intimacy ... at deeper levels.

- What do you think of when you think of intimacy?
- Some people think of intimacy as spending time together. For others, intimacy is about communicating and sharing each other's deepest feelings. For others, intimacy is all about the sexual relationship.
- Within this principle, we discuss what intimacy really is, and the importance of cultivating it at deeper levels.

Principle 3: Lift your partner ... every day.

- Do you remember the first few months with your partner? The excitement you experienced, the way you felt every time you were with them, the way you spoke to them, the things you did for each other? It was so uplifting, wasn't it?
- Then: life happens. Whether it's the work you do or the roles you play, other things may have gradually taken priority over lifting your partner up.
- If you want a lifelong honeymoon, this *has to change*. You can't let the urgency of life push aside the importance of creating magical moments every day with your partner.

Principle 4: Manage the differences ... with care and communication.

- This is the first of four principles where our focus is on preventing the negative things that break down otherwise strong relationships.
- While the statement "opposites attract" is often true when it comes to <u>initial</u> attraction, over time it's typically those same opposites that can create conflict and stress in relationships.
- From my work with hundreds of couples, I have found that there are three major differences that can cause significant challenges for couples: communication styles, love languages, and personality traits.
- In this principle we provide specific strategies for dealing with these differences.

Principle 5: Avoid the fire starters ... they can ignite a blaze.

- If you were creating a bonfire, you would want to have the right kindling to get the fire started. Unfortunately, emotional fire starters are just that, the kindling that can lead to burning down your relationship house!

- We can think of these behaviors as ways people often express their real, valid thoughts and feelings about themselves and their partner, but in such negative ways that it can be destructive.

- In this principle we identify specific behaviors (such as criticizing, blaming, shaming) that can be the start of serious breakdowns. If you want a lifelong honeymoon, you need to be diligent about avoiding these emotional fire starters.

Principle 6: Address conflict ... resolve disagreements.

- Many of us grew up in families that didn't teach how to address conflict in a healthy way. As a result, many couples are poorly equipped to handle disagreement and so respond with either fight (arguments that can cause significant attachment injuries), flight (avoiding the disagreement completely until it becomes an overwhelming crisis), or freeze (a reflex that renders one unresponsive or unable to move.

- Surprisingly, there are only three reasons people disagree. And fortunately, there are specific strategies that can be applied for addressing each.

- In this principle, we help you understand disagreements and give you the pathways to cleanly resolve them.

Principle 7: Repair the ruptures ... they can ruin you.

- While managing the differences and avoiding the fire starters are proactive ways to create your lifelong honeymoon, inevitably ruptures or hurts will occur in the relationship. How you respond to them will make all the difference in sustaining your lifelong honeymoon.

- Some ruptures will be scrapes or abrasions that occur as a result of two people who are different, and those differences rubbing against each other at no fault of either partner.

- Other ruptures will be bruises; they hurt a little more and are a direct result of one partner's action that causes a minor to moderate injury to the other.

- And still others are deep cuts; like bruises, deep cuts occur when one of the partners is at fault and harm is caused to the other partner. However, the wound is deep and potentially fatal to the relationship.

- Regardless of the type of rupture, care must be taken to repair them. In this principle we talk about the types of ruptures and how to repair each of them.

> **Just because partners love one another, that isn't enough to have the type of relationship many of the couples I've treated have described wanting.**

Principle 8: Profess, protect, and prioritize your relationship ... with your thoughts, words, and actions.

- You can think of this final principle as being all about preventive maintenance: the things you are going to do and not do on an ongoing basis to keep your lifelong honeymoon going!

- Imagine your partner in a room filled with people they find highly attractive. What would you want your partner to do to protect your relationship?

- What would you want your partner to profess about your relationship when talking to others?

- And finally, what are the things you would want you and your partner to be doing on a regular basis to ensure that you are both prioritizing the relationship?

- Your preventive maintenance steps are a vital key to living your lifelong honeymoon.

Understanding the Wheel

I want to point out several aspects of the wheel.

- Each of the eight principles is vital to creating and sustaining a lifelong honeymoon. The wheel is intended to indicate that there is NOT a rank or order of importance. We use the numbers 1–8 purely for ease in discussion.

- The colors have meaning and purpose. The first three principles are red because many couples experience these principles as the rosy, loving, fun stuff.

- Principles 5, 6, and 7 are dark gray, implying that many couples experience fire starters, conflicts, and ruptures as the more challenging times in a relationship.

- Principles 4 (Manage the differences) and 8 (Profess, protect, and prioritize) are white and help keep the peace by helping you to stay in the red zone and have more of those loving and positive experiences.

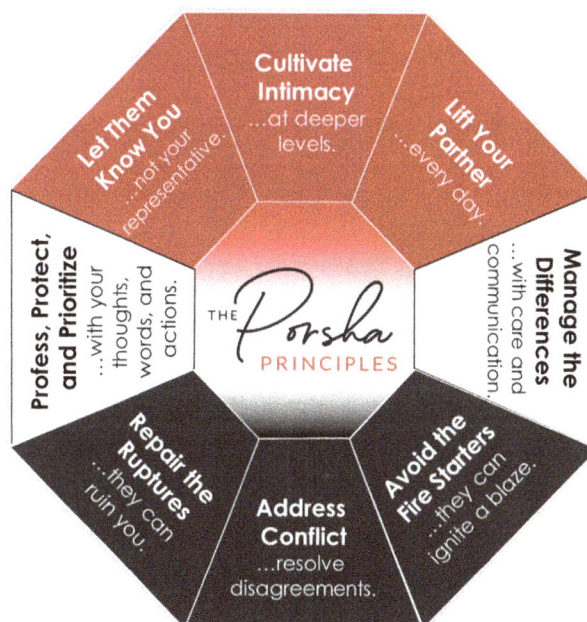

Just because partners love one another, that isn't enough to have the type of relationship many of the couples I've treated have described wanting. To live a lifelong honeymoon requires so much more. Because it is inevitable that partners will have differences, will come into the relationship with baggage, and will disappoint or hurt one another, they need to have a special set of skills and strategies to navigate through these complex challenges. The practice of these eight principals will help your love and passion steer the course, helping you to experience a lifelong honeymoon.

Since each of the eight principles are vital to creating the kind of relationship you and your partner both deserve, you may be wondering, *Where do we start?* That's up to the two of you. The principles are all interrelated and make reference to one another. Here are a few approaches to consider.

- Some couples find it helpful to start with Principle 1 and then move through the principles in order, studying one principle per week. Once they get to Principle 8, the last principle, they often find it helpful to restart again to pick up what they didn't get fully the first time.
- Other couples prefer to start first with the principle that represents their area of greatest perceived need. Perhaps it's Principle 3: Cultivate intimacy, or Principle 4: Manage the differences, or Principle 6: Address conflicts, or even Principle 7: Repair the ruptures. After mastering that principle, they then go back to Principle 1 and go through the principles in order.
- Finally, other couples find it better to bounce around from principle to principle based on their need at the time.

Whichever approach you decide on, be sure to go beyond just reviewing the material. Someone who wants to get better at tennis doesn't get better by reading a book on tennis. You get better by practicing the new approaches and strategies.

Likewise, your relationship won't improve by just learning about the Porsha Principles. You have to practice them. So do it. Do the various exercises that are included throughout the book. Practice them with your partner, get feedback, and practice some more. It's through practicing the principles that you and your partner will get on the path to building your lifelong honeymoon!

> **Your relationship won't improve by just learning about the Porsha Principles. You have to practice them. So do it.**

Practicing the Principle	**Which of the principles do you most need to work on?**
	To find out, you and your partner should take the Principles Assessment online or use the form that follows.
	<ul><li>Rate your relationship on the three questions for each principle.</li><li>If a question has multiple parts, and you believe you rate high on some parts and low on others, adjust the score appropriately.</li><li>Score each principle by adding up the rating for the three questions for that principle. For example, if you rated the three questions 3, 5, and 6, your total would be 14. Place the total in the box to the left of the principle title.</li><li>Have your partner do the same by rating and scoring using a separate copy of the assessment.</li><li>Compare scores for each of the principles. Any principle that either of you score below 15 on should be considered as a possible Principle for Focus (see the "Your Couple's Action Plan" in the Final Word section of the book).</li><li>I recommend that you NOT take on more than one or two principles at a time, to allow more time for the learning and the strategies to sink into your day-to-day routine.</li></ul>

The Principles Assessment

(The free and premium online assessments are available at www.PorshaPrinciples.com)

Total

		Strongly Disagree		Disagree		Agree		
P1: Let Them Know You … NOT Your Representative.		1	2	3	4	5	6	7
1.1 We are our authentic selves with each other.								
1.2 We avoid showing up with one of the common representatives (Silent Martyr, Pleaser, Placater, Deflector, Workaholic, Jokester, Aggressor).								
1.3 We call each other out when one of us is representing instead of being authentic.								
P2: Cultivate Intimacy … at Deeper Levels.		1	2	3	4	5	6	7
2.1 We feel very close and connected in our relationship.								
2.2 In our communication we talk about our feelings, desires, fears, and dreams.								
2.3 We are curious about each other, ask questions of one another, and seek to deeply understand each other's needs and wants.								
P3: Lift Your Partner … every Day.		1	2	3	4	5	6	7
3.1 We know each other's primary and secondary love languages.								
3.2 We consistently take steps to love our partner the way our partner wants to be loved.								
3.3 We regularly check in to ensure we are both feeling loved and lifted by the other.								
P4: Manage the Differences … with Care & Communication.		1	2	3	4	5	6	7
4.1 We have identified our major differences that impact the relationship.								
4.2 We have developed strategies and successfully use them in managing our differences.								
4.3 We are caring and considerate when we have conflict over a difference.								

The Principles Assessment

Total

	P5: Avoid the fire starters ... they can ignite a blaze.	Strongly Disagree		Disagree		Agree		
		1	2	3	4	5	6	7
	5.1 We have identified two or more things each of us do that tend to be fire starters.							
	5.2 We actively and intentionally do specific things to eliminate fire starters.							
	5.3 When a fire ignites, we quickly take steps to prevent it from becoming a blaze.							

	P6: Address conflict ... resolve disagreements.	Strongly Disagree		Disagree		Agree		
		1	2	3	4	5	6	7
	6.1 We have identified the major areas of our relationship that frequently cause disagreements between us.							
	6.2 We have determined the type and reason for our major disagreements and have identified strategies for addressing each one.							
	6.3 When disagreements occur we are proactive and employ our strategies for addressing them.							

	P7: Repair the ruptures ... they can ruin you.	Strongly Disagree		Disagree		Agree		
		1	2	3	4	5	6	7
	7.1 We have discussed and resolved past ruptures that have occurred in our relationship.							
	7.2 We have regular check-ins to ensure that scrapes, bruises, and deep cuts are identified.							
	7.3 We have agreed on strategies and use them to address ruptures that occur.							

	P8: Profess, protect, and prioritize the relationship ... with your thoughts, words, and actions.	Strongly Disagree		Disagree		Agree		
		1	2	3	4	5	6	7
	8.1 We have established boundaries in key areas to protect our relationship, and we ensure boundaries are respected.							
	8.2 We both feel that the other prioritizes our relationship.							
	8.3 We regularly speak positively about our partner in front of our family, friends, and work associates.							

Notes

Principle 1:
Let Them Know You ... NOT Your Representative

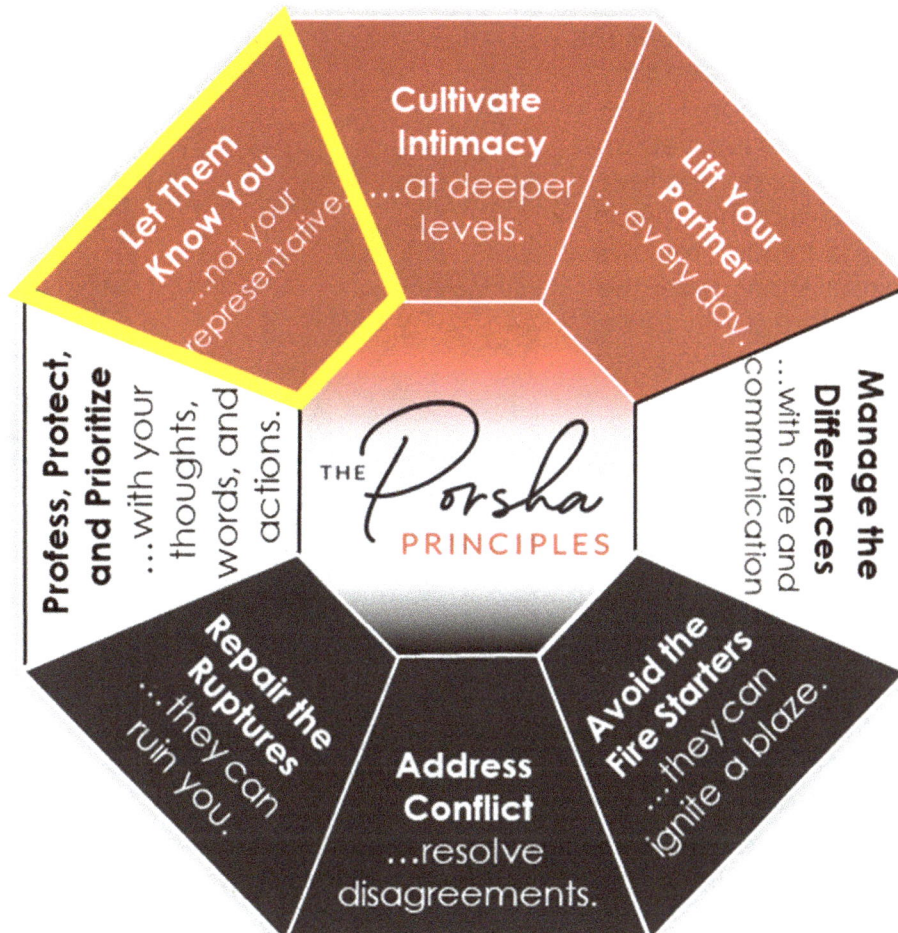

The Porsha Principles diagram showing:
- Let Them Know You ...not your representative.
- Cultivate Intimacy ...at deeper levels.
- Lift Your Partner ...every day.
- Manage the Differences ...with care and communication
- Avoid the Fire Starters ...they can ignite a blaze.
- Address Conflict ...resolve disagreements.
- Repair the Ruptures ...they can ruin you.
- Profess, Protect, and Prioritize ...with your thoughts, words, and actions.

What You Will Learn	
	Foundation • What is a representative? • Why do we create them? • Why are they harmful? **Proactive** • How to prevent representatives from showing up **Intervention** • How to intervene when you suspect your partner's representative has taken over **Action** • Steps you and your partner can take to put the principle into practice: "Parts of Me"

Introduction

I remember when I first spoke over the phone with Michael, the man with whom I am spending my lifelong honeymoon. I have to confess: I was a bit guarded and reserved. I knew of quite a few not-so-great relationships among my friends and through my own personal experiences. Over the phone I presented a very polite and professional, but somewhat distant and self-reliant, personality. I made sure I was fully pursued. I refused to show any of my emotional "cards." There was no way I was going to get played or hurt. I was like Fort Knox: he had to have the "secret code" to penetrate my armor, my representative, to get closer to the real me.

- But when he met me in person on the first date, he says he immediately saw through that tough phone exterior and could see the warm and loving person I really was! He still teases me about it to this day. For him, my smile said it all!

- I tried my hardest to keep my guard up for weeks, but his persistence, transparency, and consistency wore my guard down.

- Later I went back and thought about all the time and energy I put into this "representative" of mine: the evasiveness and the "push forward/pull back" behaviors that I demonstrated. At the time they felt like an armor of protection that would keep me safe. While it was worth it to feel the armor's protection early on, he would never have fallen in love with me if I hadn't show him my true self and allowed our bond to deepen.

- And worse, if he had fallen in love with my representative, perhaps because he preferred a surface relationship, and then later learned that I was someone who desired a deep level of intimacy from the man in my life, this could have spelled disaster for both of us—because neither of our needs would have been met!

Representatives typically aren't sustainable, and someone will get let down or feel fooled when the real you is revealed. I've seen partners in long-term, committed relationships still employ representatives to hide their vulnerabilities and insecurities. In essence, we set up our relationships for failure right from the beginning by not letting the other person know the real us. We can actually increase the probability that the relationship will fail with this very approach! In fact, I almost lost my man in those first few months by keeping my protection up and holding back how I truly felt.

So, when it comes to relationships, whether you are in the beginning of one or have been married for decades, there are important questions to answer when it comes to dealing with representatives and keeping them in check.

Let's get into these questions now, starting with what is a representative?

What is a Representative?

> **Your representative is any projection of yourself that is outside the transparency of your true, authentic self.**

Your representative is any projection of yourself that is outside the transparency of your true, authentic self. It is an attempt to project a picture of yourself that is different from the truth, in order to give your partner or others a more favorable view of you.

Why Do We Create Representatives?

While I was putting up my representative for protection, other people put up their representatives for other reasons.

- Some people may struggle with how they see themselves and fear others will see their deficits too.
- Some people may fear rejection, hold back, and avoid making the first real move.
- Some use a representative to cover up, or avoid addressing, issues or emotions.
- Some show a representative intentionally for selfish reasons to take advantage of others.

In a world where we are expected to fit in and be good enough in every area of our lives and make everyone happy or get rejected, it makes sense that we wouldn't want to show the most vulnerable parts of ourselves, the failing parts of ourselves, to our partners for fear of disappointment and disconnection.

How Do Representatives Show Up?

Early on in relationships when partners are trying to fit in and measure up, representatives typically show up in two ways.

- **Doing things that you WOULD NOT normally do**
  Examples
  - Dressing provocatively when you normally dress conservatively when you go out
  - Going to church every Sunday when you normally go about three times a year … in a good year: Easter, Christmas, and New Year's

- Working out regularly when you know you are a couch potato
- Buying expensive gifts when you can't afford it
- Doing adventurous outdoor things when you know you are scared of bugs and prefer staying in

- **NOT doing things that you WOULD normally do**

Examples

- Not using profanity even though it is regularly part of your vocabulary
- Staying home watching television when you prefer to be out partying most weekends
- Not spending time with friends and family when typically they take up a huge part of your time
- Not spending Sundays watching the game, even though you are an avid sports fan
- Not letting your partner know how much religion or spirituality is an important part of your life
- Not showing your partner your typical alcohol or drug use

Representatives Later in the Relationship

After you get past your partner's initial representative, to sustain your lifelong honeymoon it's even more important that you stay diligent and aware of the more difficult task: spotting representatives after you feel you've gotten to know your partner really well.

Sample Representatives
- Silent Martyr
- Workaholic
- Pleaser
- Jokester
- Placater
- Aggressor
- Deflector

Here are a few examples of how a representative may show up later in your relationship:

- **Silent Martyr**: You keep quiet, instead of vocalizing your concerns.
- **Pleaser**: You constantly please your partner to get them to love you.
- **Placater**: You tell your partner what they want to hear instead of your true feelings.
- **Deflector**: You avoid addressing your own issues by focusing the conversation on other issues.
- **Workaholic**: You keep busy to avoid addressing emotions or problems
- **Jokester**: You use humor or sarcasm to cover up other feelings.
- **Aggressor**: You are quick to pick a fight to avoid addressing the real issues.

Keep in mind that some of these behaviors can appear to show up at appropriate times to respond to a life circumstance. For example, someone who has a huge work project due and is working around the clock to meet the deadline may be working long hours during that period. But that's not a workaholic as I have defined it. That is, they are not keeping "busy to avoid addressing emotions or problems." The point is that when these behaviors show up in order to cover up or hide another issue, then they serve as representatives.

What follows is a section we call, "Deeper Dive." The purpose of a deeper dive is to provide an opportunity to uncover potential deeper causes of the behaviors and motivations that you and your partner demonstrate. These are the types of questions that may be better explored with a therapist. We offer them here as a vehicle for you to begin thinking deeper about how your history impacts how you are showing up in your relationship.

While we often may have automatic negative reactions to some of the things our partner might say or do, understanding the root causes of your behavior can empower you to disrupt those automatic reactions and replace them with more authentic and empathetic responses.

Deeper Dive

Some people may find that their representatives are rooted in their history or how they grew up. For example, a person who is a pleaser may discover when they look back that they had a very critical parent who had a low tolerance for mistakes. Or someone who is a silent martyr may think back and recall that when growing up, most needs or requests they made would be met with upsetting or dismissive comments from their parents or primary caregivers.

Consider exploring these deeper questions which may help you get to the roots of your representatives and why you created them.
- What roles did your parents, or primary caregivers, play in your household (e.g., disciplinarian, encourager, bread winner, caretaker)?
- What were the various roles you played growing up based on your personality or your family's dynamics or situation (e.g., rebel, tattletale, bully, scapegoat, victim, **invisible person**, golden child, **money provider**)?
- How did you show up in those roles (i.e., what did you do to carry those roles out)?
- What were the things that motivated your behavior when in those roles (e.g., the desire to please, the desire to win, the desire to be helpful, etc.)?
- What rewards did you receive for playing these roles? What were the consequences?
- How did playing these roles make you feel?
- How do these same roles and motivations show up in your life today?

With this understanding, how might you begin showing up differently—in a more authentic way that reflects your true self?

Sample Dialogue: The Representative

Let's take a look at Pam and Marcus in their early years, and Marcus' representative in action.

Pam: Honey, I've been saving my money all year and want to take a two-week European tour in a few months. I would love for you to go with me. What do you think?

Marcus: Sure, it'll be great!

Actually, Marcus doesn't have the money for the trip, but he doesn't want to admit it and risk Pam seeing him as broke. His self-doubt and insecurity kicks in. So he employs his representative, the placater, and agrees to go.

Instead of the placater a different representative might show up. For example, the deflector might appear to deflect attention away from his real concern about the expense:

- *I've heard that Europe is way overpriced and not at all worth it.*
- *You don't want to go to Europe; it's just not worth your time right now.*
- *We'll see, but let's go ahead and order dinner.*

Let's fast forward. Let's say they actually go on the trip that Marcus really couldn't afford to go on. What might his representative, the Aggressor, now do after he's overspent on this trip?

- Express irritation (*I didn't want to go on this trip in the first place*).
- Look for things to complain about.
- Erupt with anger at trivial things.

Can you hear the bait and switch here? Marcus happily agreed to go on the trip with Pam, but then is irritable and complains the whole time, all because he let his representative take over instead of being honest about his concern over the expense.

Authenticity: A Key to Your Lifelong Honeymoon

> **Authenticity means being genuine, transparent, and truthful with yourself and with others about who you are.**

What is authenticity and why is it crucial to a relationship, and why do we find it so hard to demonstrate? Professor Brene Brown, a vulnerability and shame researcher and author of *The Gifts of Imperfection*, describes authenticity as the daily practice of letting go of who we think we are supposed to be and embracing who we are. She goes on to say it's a conscious choice of how we want to live.

Authenticity means being genuine, transparent, and truthful with yourself and with others about who you are. When you are not authentic, when you don't show your partner the real you, your partner isn't having a relationship with you, they're having a relationship with your representative.

Authenticity is certainly scary, but if you are not real and the other person falls in love with your representative, how strong can that love be? How long can that "love" last?

What Can Happen When You Are Not Authentic?

- Sometimes you will feel like an imposter. You may feel fear and anxiety that your partner might discover the real you. You may feel pressure to keep up that representative.
- Other times, the other person may be turned off by the representative, and you may lose a potential partner.
- Your partner may be supporting the needs of the representative, instead of your true needs, and YOU end up walking away with your needs unmet.
- Sometimes when your partner discovers the real you they may be disappointed.

But when you are authentic and let your partner know who you really are and how you really feel, you allow your partner to support you and keep falling in love with the real you, cultivating a lifelong honeymoon.

Who's "Reppin'" You?

We all have different parts of ourselves that make up our whole, and that is completely normal. However, partners often employ one of their representatives in an attempt to cover up an underlying insecurity or vulnerability. This lack of authenticity can get in the way of sustaining your lifelong honeymoon. I believe knowing oneself at a deep level aids in one's ability to be authentic. It can also help you spot your representatives quicker.

> **Partners often employ one of their representatives in an attempt to cover up an underlying insecurity or vulnerability.**

Early on in our relationship, Michael did a pretty unusual thing. To help me better understand him and his most authentic self, he told me about six different parts of himself that made up his whole. He even had names for them! Of course, as a therapist and because Michael was my romantic interest, I was intrigued. I wanted to know more so I could know him on a much deeper level. The box on the next page shows how Michael described his six different parts.

Personal Insight	**The Parts of Michael**
	• **James**. At times, James is driving my bus. In the Bible, James said "Faith without works is dead." (James 2:14-26, King James Version) My James gets things done. He is a hard worker and loves accomplishing things. When I am being led by James, my first thoughts in the morning are about what I am going to get done that day.
	• **Preston**. Impressive Preston loves being out front. Whether impressing people with his own ideas and viewpoints or using his facilitation skills to help bring out the views and thoughts of others, he loves leading and guiding. While James pushes me to get things done, Preston wants to make sure I get appropriate credit for it!
	• **Carl**. Critical Carl is the side of me that judges everything and everybody. Carl thinks everyone can be better and everything can be done better. He naturally finds fault in people and situations and wants to offer his thoughts on how things should be improved. His first thought in the morning: *Let's get this stuff fixed*.
	• **Tony**. My sensual self is Tony. Tony likes anything and everything sensual. Tony loves the female form, loves being flirtatious, loves the sexual sensations. He loves giving pleasure and receiving it. Tony's first thought: *What's going to feel good today?*
	• **Mikey**. Little Mikey is the insecure little boy who in a crowded room can become so self-conscious that he shrinks down to nothing. When Mikey is driving my bus I find myself becoming an observer, a non-participant who becomes focused on how inadequate I am because I have nothing to say and nothing to contribute. It reminds me of times in my teenage years when I was ridiculed, and I sometimes forget that I am not that little boy anymore.
	• **Michael**. There are times in my life when I strongly desire to follow God. I strongly want to listen for God's promptings. I call this my "Michael," because "Michael" means "he who is like God." When Michael is driving my bus, my first thoughts in the morning are about getting quiet and meditating. I find myself expressing warmth and love toward everyone.

When Michael sat down and described to me his authentic self with all of these parts, I understood him much more and felt closer to him. As our relationship grew, we would joke about, "It looks like Critical Carl is out today, what's going on with you?" or "I could use a little more of Tony right now…."

Keep in mind, although these parts work together wonderfully most of the time, when self-doubt or insecurity seeps in, one of them can rear its head as a representative hiding what is truly the issue. As an example, if Michael was nervous or experiencing self-doubt about the impression he would make on our first date, Preston could have been out of control with trying to show me how "great" he was. You can imagine if that had happened, there would not have been a second date!

After talking with Michael about his authentic self, it influenced me to look at myself more fully and name the different parts of me. Trust me, we all have different parts of ourselves and that's normal! It's these parts that make up the whole. I was quickly able to identify that it was "Paula the Protector" who was "reppin'" me when I first met Michael because of my own fears and insecurities. She was the one who put up the guard and pretended to be tough and in charge. Who was she protecting? "Porshey," the soft and loving part of me whose caring ways had been taken advantage of on too many occasions. And so on and so on ... hopefully you are catching on so you can name the authentic parts of yourself too!

Proactive Strategies

How do you prevent the representative from showing up? Below are five strategies that you can use.

1. Take a first step toward practicing authenticity: challenge yourself to share something real about yourself with your partner that you haven't shared before.

2. Strive to be open and honest with your partner on a regular basis about your deepest thoughts and feelings. Tell your partner about your hopes, fears, dreams, and concerns.

3. As you evolve, let your partner know how you have grown and changed as a person. Let them know your new needs and how they can support you.

4. Do the "Parts of Me" exercise with your partner that appears at the end of this section to uncover and reveal the many parts of yourself.

5. Determine if you are truly ready to love.
   - Many of us have the habit of dating the "same person" over and over again—the names change but the result is always the same. This often happens because we haven't recognized our own unhealthy relationship patterns and haven't developed new ones.
   - Talk this out with safe friends who really know you and know your hang-ups and strengths.
   - If necessary, seek therapy to identify and resolve unhealthy relationship patterns.

Intervention Strategies

What should you do if you catch yourself "representing"?
   - Immediately acknowledge it, take responsibility, and reset.

- *I'm sorry, that's not what I really meant to say…. Let me be completely honest here…*

- Dig deeper and be brave. Share your real feelings and insecurities with you partner.
  - *What I am really feeling is …*
  - *What is hard for me to say is …*
- Ask specifically for what you want.
  - *It would be helpful to me if you would …*

What should you do if you catch your partner "representing"?

- Immediately acknowledge it and request a reset.
  - *I hear your words. But from the way you … it seems like something else may be going on here. Would you take a second and consider if there is something else you really want to say?*
- Use your assertive communication and reflective listening skills to help your partner express their authentic thoughts and feelings. In Principle 4, Managing the differences, we describe the assertive communication and reflective listening approaches, as summarized below.
  - Use reflective listening to play back what you heard or saw.
    - *It sounds like what you are saying is …*
  - Use I-statements with feeling words.
    - *When you are holding back and not sharing, I feel …*
  - Ask specifically for what you need.
    - *It would be helpful to me if you would …*

Once your partner takes a step toward practicing authenticity with you, make sure you respond with emotional responsiveness. Below are a few examples:

- Make your partner feel heard by using reflective listening to restate what you heard.
- Validate their fears.
  - *I can see why you feel that way.*
- Acknowledge their vulnerability with compassion and empathy.
  - Express comforting words
  - Hug your partner
- Get curious by asking follow-up questions.
  - *Can you tell me more about that?*

Back to Pam and Marcus

Let's take a look at how the conversation between Pam and Marcus could have gone if Marcus was practicing authenticity.

Pam: Honey, I've been saving my money all year and want to take a two-week European tour in a few months. I would love for you to go with me. What do you think?

Marcus:	That sounds like a great trip, and I would love to go with you. I need to take a look at my finances to make sure it's something I can make happen.
Pam:	Oh, I totally get that. I've been saving for months and realize now I should have mentioned it months ago. But hey, I got a bonus coming up and if you find it's a stretch, I can probably help.

Now, in the second scenario, if Marcus had gone on the trip without revealing his true concern and found himself feeling resentful about being on the trip, he might say:

Marcus:	I recognize that I am feeling a little cranky because I agreed to go on the trip even though my budget was tight. But now that we are here, I need your help because I really do want to make this a great time for both of us. So, if you sense me being cranky, would you remind me, "Do you need a minute?"

Summary and Close

Let's recap what we covered in this principle.

- We started with talking about what a representative is, why we create them, and the damage they can cause by presenting a false image of who we are.
- We defined authenticity and explained the vital role authenticity plays in creating your lifelong honeymoon.
- We introduced the concept of "Who's reppin' you," a framework for thinking about the different parts that make up each of us.
- Finally, we covered proactive strategies and intervention strategies: things to do when you or your partner are representing instead of being your authentic selves.

The exercise that follows, "The Parts of Me," gives you and your partner an opportunity to better understand the different parts of each other. Being authentic by showing who you really are is indeed a critical step for building a foundation of openness, vulnerability, and acceptance that will serve you well in creating and sustaining your lifelong honeymoon.

Practicing the Principle	**Parts of Me** • The purpose of this activity is to identify and give names to the different parts of you that show up in your relationship. • We recommend that you and your partner first work individually on your own parts. Then come together to share the information and get suggestions and additional insights from each other. • Follow the directions on the next page.

Parts of Me

The purpose of this activity is to identify and give names to the different parts of you that show up in your relationship. Identifying the parts can increase your awareness of who is repping each of you at any given time, allowing the two of you to respond more appropriately as needed.

We recommend that you and your partner first work individually on your own parts. Then come together to share the information and get suggestions and additional insights from each other. Do keep in mind that for this exercise each person is the authority on themselves. While the partner can offer thoughts to consider, each individual makes the final decision on what their parts are and what to call them.

To identify potential parts of yourself, consider the following.
- First, look back at the descriptions of the different parts of Michael and Porsha.
- Next, think about the different roles you play, such as husband/wife, parent, worker, neighbor, tennis player, etc.
- Think about what you feel society, your partner, and others expect of you and what additional roles you play to meet those expectations.
- Think about how you show up in those roles and **the things that motivate your behavior** when in those roles (e.g., the desire to please, the desire to win, the desire to be helpful, etc.)
- Consider times when you show up less than the amazing person that you are naturally. Think about what is **motivating your behavior** during those times.
- With these thoughts in mind, what might be different parts of you that show up at different times?

In the diagram, place your name in the center. The names of the parts go on each spoke. Add additional spokes if needed. Consider using catchy names that will help you remember, such as Critical Carl or Pam the Protector.

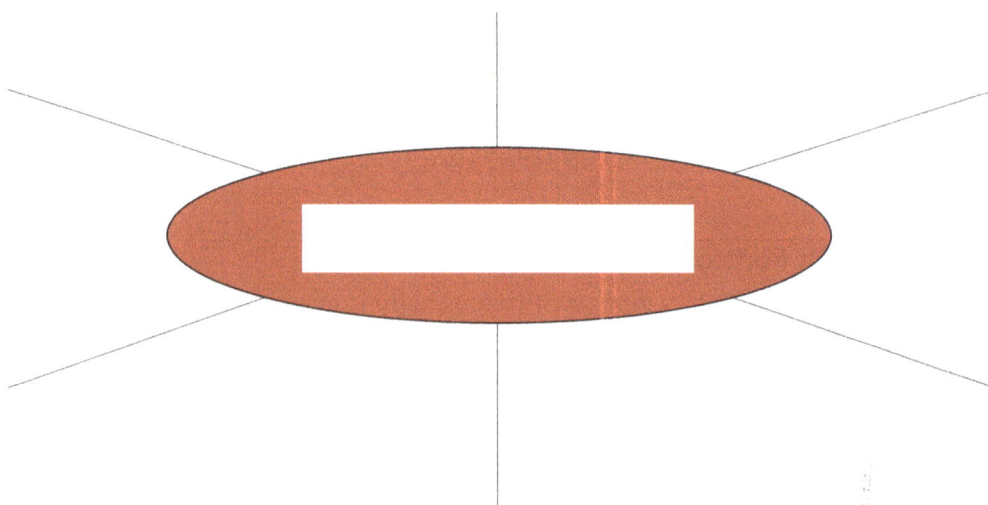

Notes

Notes

Principle 2:
Cultivate Intimacy ... at Deeper Levels

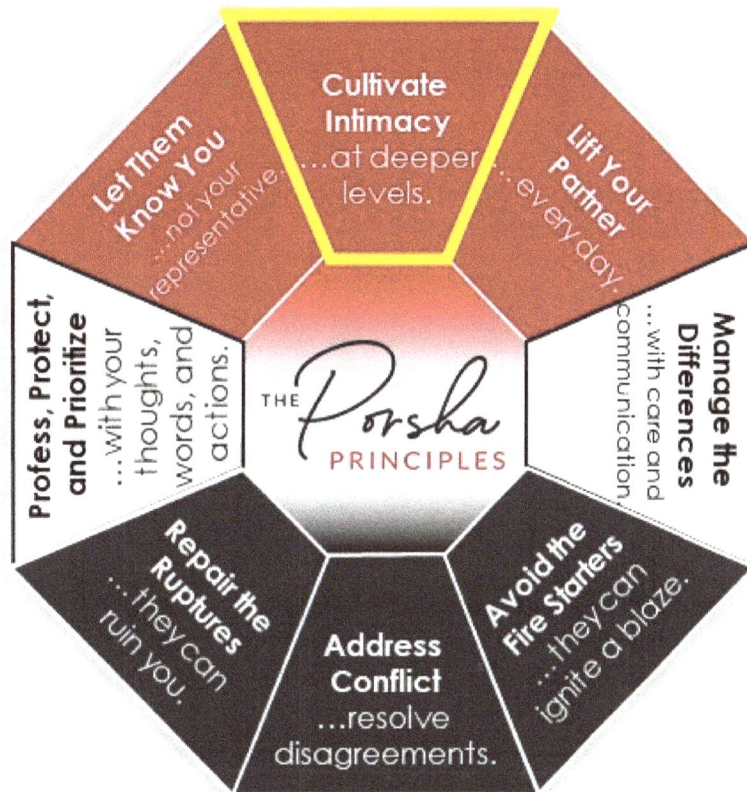

What You Will Learn	**Foundation** • What is intimacy and what are the three S's of intimacy? • What happens when you don't have intimacy? • What does it mean to have intimacy in all areas of your life? • How do you assess the depth of intimacy in your relationship? • Why aren't deeper levels of intimacy achieved in some relationships? • The three keys for deeper intimacy • Prerequisites for an uplifting and fulfilling sexual relationship **Proactive Strategies** • Five strategies to establish a pattern of healthy intimacy **Intervention Strategies** • Three strategies to employ should intimacy break down **Action** • Steps you and your partner can take to put the principle into practice: The Intimacy Game

Introduction

What is intimacy? What happens when you don't have intimacy? And what does it mean to cultivate it at deeper levels in the relationship? Let's pick back up with Pam and Marcus.

- Early in their relationship, Pam and Marcus found themselves being deeply engaged in conversations concerning just about anything and everything.

- Marcus was intrigued to hear stories about how Pam put herself through grad school after her parents lost their business during a recession. He laughed with her as she described going through nearly a year on baked beans and Ramen noodles.

- When he asked her about how it felt to be such a strong and resilient woman, she actually had to think about it because no man had ever seen her that way. She had never really let anyone see the sacrifices and hurts that it took to achieve success.

- He also asked her about what kept her so driven. It hadn't occurred to her before, but deep inside she didn't want to let her parents down. Thinking about it made her eyes well up with tears.

- Marcus reached out and embraced her. He told her that it must have been so hard for her and that she should be so proud of herself for her success.

- When she looked back on it a year later, she realized it was in that moment that she began to feel closer to him, and that was the start of deeper and more intimate conversations to come.

Intimacy is a powerful thing and can bond a couple strongly. In fact, this story demonstrates **three key elements of intimacy**, which I call the 3 S's.

- Someone sharing
- Someone seeking
- Someone supporting

We will talk more about the 3 S's of intimacy later, but first let's get into definitions.

What Is Intimacy?

We define intimacy as a feeling of closeness, support, and emotional connection. With intimacy comes the ability and awareness to share a deep range of thoughts and feelings with each other. Intimacy involves a practice of being open and vulnerable, letting your guard down, and revealing your past, your present, your hopes, and your dreams.

> **Intimacy is a feeling of closeness, support, and emotional connection.**

Cultivating intimacy with someone you love can be one of the most rewarding aspects of a relationship. However, deeper levels of intimacy happen only once trust and communication between two people are at a high level, a level that fosters the mutual sharing of one another's deepest selves. As a result, intimacy is typically built up over time, and so it requires patience and effort from both partners to cultivate and sustain.

What Happens When You Don't Have Intimacy?

When you don't have an adequate depth of intimacy in your relationship, you may hear things like this from your partner.

- *I don't understand you ...*
- *You never listen to me ...*
- *You just don't get me ...*
- *Sometimes I don't think I really know you at all ...*
- *Why can't you just be happy with ...*
- *I feel completely alone ...*
- *I can't go on like this ...*

When I hear the panic, sadness, and hopelessness in phrases like these in my couple therapy sessions, it's a very strong indication that the couple is having an intimacy breakdown. Research[2] studies have shown that connection and intimacy are correlated with better overall emotional and physical health and elevated immune responses. Lack of intimacy can result in couples feeling desperately alone and unfulfilled, putting them at a higher risk for mental health disorders.

---

[2] Sarah Stewart-Brown, "Emotional well-being and its relation to health: Physical disease may well result from emotional distress." *British Medical Journal*, Dec. 12, 1998, 1608–1609.

What Does It Mean to Have Intimacy in All Areas?

There are many areas in a relationship for developing intimacy. I want to focus on these five in particular. In my work I have found that these five tend to form the pillars of a strong, long-term, fulfilling relationship.

- Emotional intimacy
- Sexual intimacy
- Physical intimacy (i.e., touch and affection)
- Spiritual intimacy
- Financial intimacy

I like using the iceberg analogy to describe three depths of intimacy: surface, shallow, and deep.

- Many couples' intimacy stops at the tip of the iceberg. Their interaction is at the surface level, and they fail to connect with the depth of their partner because they don't ask and learn about meaningful thoughts and feelings that lie beneath the surface.
- Other couples get under the surface and into the shallow depths of intimacy, but often shy away from the deeper discussions to avoid conflict, strong emotions (theirs or their partners), or uncomfortable conversations.
- However, couples who regularly demonstrate vulnerability, support for their partner, and a willingness to openly communicate, are typically able to move into deeper and more fulfilling depths of intimacy.

The depth of intimacy a couple has can vary across the five areas of intimacy. For example, a couple's level of intimacy may be deep in some areas but surface in others.

How Do You Assess the Depth of Intimacy in Your Relationship?

The table on the next page gives examples of what intimacy might look like for each area across the three levels. Note that it is not unusual for couples to find that they haven't yet achieved even the surface depth of intimacy in one or more areas.

Can you have a lifelong honeymoon without having Level-3 intimacy in all areas? Of course you can. Couples can intuitively "know" the wants and needs of one another without the deep level of intimacy indicated in the table. However, in my experience, **it is far more often the case that unspoken desires can become unfulfilled needs.** And, unfortunately, unfulfilled needs can drain the love pool.

Intimacy: Sample Areas and Level

Emotional Intimacy

Level 1: Surface	Level 2: Shallow	Level 3: Deep
We primarily talk about our day and the practical things we need to talk about to get through life.	We mostly talk about our day and the practical things we need to talk about to get through life. At times we do go deeper to understand why, how we felt, our hopes, and our fears. *Note: Stressful events can trigger going beyond the surface level.*	Our conversations frequently go beyond the things of the day. We often delve into why we did them and how we felt about them. We easily discuss our hopes and dreams, as well as our fears and concerns.

Sexual Intimacy

Level 1: Surface	Level 2: Shallow	Level 3: Deep
We have talked about sex but have not become sexually intimate.	We have an established sexual routine. We seldom talk about whether it is satisfying, how to make it better, or our sexual fantasies.	We talk about and understand each other's sexual experiences, needs, and fantasies, and we regularly seek to fulfill one another's sexual desires.

Physical Intimacy *(i.e., touch and affection)*

Level 1: Surface	Level 2: Shallow	Level 3: Deep
We have infrequent physical contact and rarely verbally express words of love and affection to one another.	We have routine physical contact and routinely speak words of affection but at predictable times and with predictable frequency.	We understand each other's need for touch and affection and are intentional about providing the level needed for our partner's fulfillment.

Spiritual Intimacy		
Level 1: Surface	**Level 2: Shallow**	**Level 3: Deep**
We are aware of each other's spiritual and religious beliefs, but seldom have conversations or shared experiences.	We have occasional discussions about spiritual topics and sometimes share in a spiritual or religious experience.	We frequently spend time together talking about spiritual topics and regularly participate together in spiritual or religious experiences.

Financial Intimacy		
Level 1: Surface	**Level 2: Shallow**	**Level 3: Deep**
We know each other's regular sources of income but don't know amounts or overall financial status.	We know each other's financial status, as well as regular sources of income and amounts.	We know each other's financial status, as well as regular sources and amounts, and have access to each other's accounts.

What Are the Keys to Achieving a Deeper Level of Intimacy?

Three keys for deeper intimacy are:

- **Vulnerability**: <u>Sharing</u> your deepest thoughts and feelings, especially when it is hard to do
- **Curiosity**: <u>Seeking</u> to know your partner in a deeper, real way by asking questions
- **Acceptance**: <u>Supporting</u> your partner emotionally in their sharing without judging, dismissing, or diminishing their experience

Why Aren't Deeper Levels of Intimacy Achieved?

Just as these are keys to intimacy, they can also explain in many cases why deeper levels of intimacy aren't achieved.

- The unwillingness to be vulnerable can be a showstopper to intimacy. When one or both partners continue to operate with their representative and don't allow themselves to be truly seen by their partner, it becomes a block to intimacy.
- In other cases, curiosity is missing. One or the other partner doesn't truly have an interest in deeper levels of intimacy, or lacks the communication skills needed, as evidenced by NOT asking their partner self-disclosing questions that encourage deeper levels of knowing.

- Or it may be that early in the relationship when intimate sharing was done by one partner, the other partner's judgment or lack of acceptance messaged that sharing intimate thoughts would likely be met with negativity.

> **To achieve the deepest level of intimacy, healthy communication is a must.**

Keep in mind that the foundation of intimacy is communication. The 3 S's—sharing, seeking, and support—rely on effective communication. For some couples, communication is key to the relationship; but for other couples, communication IS the relationship. For you and your partner, the quality of the communication measures the strength of the relationship. Therefore, to achieve the deepest level of intimacy, healthy communication is a must.

Deeper Dive

You may find it easier to be vulnerable and allow others to know you in some areas, but not in others. The cause of these differences may be rooted in your experiences growing up.

Consider using these additional questions to examine potential causes for challenges to the deepening of intimacy in your relationship.

1. Emotional intimacy
   a. What level of emotional closeness did you have with your family growing up?
2. Sexual intimacy
   a. How was sex talked about in your family (e.g., open discussion vs. avoidance; positive subject vs. negative/shaming)
3. Physical intimacy
   a. How affectionate (both verbal and physical) was your family growing up?
   b. How did you feel about the affection you received growing up?
4. Spiritual intimacy
   a. To what extent did your family have spiritual or religious beliefs and practices?
5. Financial intimacy
   a. What was the socio-economic status of your family?
   b. How did you feel about it and how did it affect your life?

How did your experiences growing up impact how you deal with each of these areas today?

So, What about the Sex Thing?

Sex is an important part of intimacy for many couples, but also can be an area of significant challenge. Therefore, I want to address this specifically.

For many partners sexual intimacy can be a powerful outward expression of the love they feel for one another. The giving and receiving of sexual pleasure can be a source of passion that energizes and uplifts the relationship.

Yet for others the sexual component of the relationship can be fraught with frustration, power struggles, and feelings of being used. For these people, the idea of sex with their partner can bring, on a good day, a sense of apathy, and on a bad day a sense of distain or dread.

My experience with hundreds of couples over my career has led me to conclude that to create and sustain a sexual relationship that is uplifting and fulfilling for both partners requires that each feels valued, supported, safe, desired, and, perhaps most importantly, cared for.

How do you achieve this? It will depend both on your needs and the needs of your partner. This will differ for every couple. However, I have found that there is a set of prerequisites—the things that must be in place to achieve a sexual relationship that is uplifting and fulfilling for both partners

Prerequisites for an Uplifting and Fulfilling Sexual Relationship
1. An unselfish desire to fulfill each other's needs
2. The openness to share and the willingness to listen
3. An all-out commitment to the ongoing learning process of adapting, giving and taking feedback, and adapting again, and then again

With these prerequisites in place, you and your partner can discuss and understand one another's sexual preferences and come to a conclusion on how to address some of the major questions surrounding sex.
- How fast would you prefer to introduce sex into our relationship?
- How frequently do you generally desire sex?
- What are the things that get you in the mood for sex?
- What are the things that break the mood for sex for you?
- What are your preferences when having sex? What most turns you on?
- What role would you want sex toys, pornography, or other sex aids to play in our sex life?
- What have been past traumas for you, if any, related to sex?
- Overall, how do we address our sexual differences?

What do you do if YOU meet all three prerequisites for an uplifting and fulfilling sexual relationship, but you feel your partner doesn't?

> **What if YOU meet all three prerequisites for an uplifting and fulfilling sexual relationship, but you feel your partner doesn't?**

If your partner is not interested in seeking to fulfill your needs, or if your partner is not willing to share their needs or hear yours, or if your partner is not willing to give and receive feedback, or adapt to learnings, it will be extremely difficult to achieve the level of sexual relationship that is uplifting and fulfilling for both of you.

If this is the case in your relationship, it may be time to enter couples therapy to address and resolve the blocks that are standing in your way. While this is not a service we provide at Porsha Principles, on our website you will find trusted referral partners who may be able to help. CLICK

Proactive Strategies

Regardless of the intimacy area, what are things that you can do right away to deepen the level of intimacy in your relationship? I want to suggest five strategies in particular.

1. **Daily seeking**. Make daily time for you and you partner to check in with one another at an intimate level. Make sure the conversation goes beyond, "How was your day?" Seek to understand your partner's present dreams, desires, and wishes, and learn how to increase your support for them. Here are questions you may find helpful to move the conversation to a deeper level of intimacy.

   - What are your hopes and dreams for your future?
   - How can I help support you in them?
   - What's been on your mind today?
   - How did that make you feel?
   - Why is that important to you?
   - What did you take away from...?
   - What do you wish you had done about...?

2. **Proactive sharing**. Be proactive in disclosing your own thoughts and feelings. As examples:
   - When your partner does something that you like, go beyond "Thank you," or "That was nice." Be specific about what you liked and why you liked it. This additional information deepens intimacy and your partner's knowledge of what's important to you and why.
   Example
   I really liked it when you brought flowers today. It makes me know that you think about me even when we are apart.
   - When your partner does something that you don't like, don't ignore the behavior or stop at, "I didn't like that." Instead, let your partner know how it made you feel and why.

Example

You promised that you would make time for you and me tonight, but you spent two hours talking with your girlfriends on the phone about your day. That makes me feel sad because your actions say to me that my desires are not that important to you.

- If you have been churning on something and you realize you have been keeping it to yourself, don't continue churning. Instead, turn to your partner and share what's been on your mind.

Example

Hey, I may have seemed a bit distracted lately. There's something that's been bothering me that I want to share with you because I can use your help in thinking it through.

3. **Supportive response**. When your partner does share an intimate thought, a supportive response is often necessary to promote further deepening of your intimacy. Here is a quick list of dos and don'ts:

Dos	Don'ts
• Give your undivided attention to your partner. • Listen intently, without interrupting, to understand your partner's thoughts and feelings. • Validate your partner with words such as, "I can see why you would feel that way," or "I would feel that way too." • Empathize with and support your partner by saying things like, "That must have been hard for you…" or "Is there anything I can do?"	• Don't ignore your partner by turning away or refusing to comment. • Don't judge or shame your partner by, for example, saying "That's stupid," or "I can't believe you did that." • Don't "should" on your partner with words that say to them, "You should have done this," or "You shouldn't have done that." • Don't blame your partner, such as saying "It's your fault," or "You got what you deserved."

4. **Connection rituals**. Be intentional about making memories by creating rituals of connection to increase your level of trust, reliance, and predictability with each other. With higher levels of trust, you and your partner will likely feel more comfortable with going to deeper levels of intimacy. Your connection rituals might include activities such as the following.

- Morning coffee time
- Mid-day "thinking of you" texts
- Occasional special sex dates
- Weekly date night out
- Working on a scrap book documenting your travels

- Holiday trips
- "Cuddle quickies"

5. **Intentional acts of love**. Recognize what makes your partner feel close to you and give that gift to them as a way of deepening intimacy. For example, for your partner the key might be praising them, touching them, giving something to them, doing something for them, or just spending time with them. Whatever it is for your partner, be intentional about giving them what they need to feel close. (When we talk about lifting your partner in Principle 3, we will more thoroughly discuss love languages and how to ensure your partner is feeling loved.)

Intervention Strategies

While the proactive strategies are things you can do in advance to establish a pattern of healthy intimacy, intervention strategies may be necessary should intimacy break down or when there is a rupture that needs repair. I want to focus on three strategies in particular that align with times when you or your partner is not sharing, not seeking, or not supporting.

1. **Not Sharing: When your partner doesn't want to engage**
   What do you do if your partner often appears distant or refuses to have a conversation at anything other than a surface level?

   - Use your healthy communication skills to let your partner know how important it is to you that you really know them, and how it makes you feel shut out and alone when they don't share their thoughts and feelings.

     Example

     It is important to me that I really know you. I feel shut out and alone when you ignore me and don't share what you're thinking.

   - When they know that you are hurting, rather than just complaining about their behavior, there is a much higher probability that they will turn toward you and become open to sharing.

2. **Not Seeking: If your partner doesn't seek to know you**
   If your partner doesn't ask questions about you or seems to lose interest when you are sharing about yourself.

   - Let your partner know about your observation and how it makes you feel.

     Example

     It seems that you don't ask questions about me and at times when I am sharing about me, you seem to lose interest or change the conversation back to you. I suspect you don't mean to do it, but it leaves me feeling unimportant and that you are not that interested in knowing me and how I feel about things. And I need you to do this for me to feel close to you.

3. **Not Supporting: If you or your partner becomes critical**
   - If YOU become critical, here is an action to consider.
     - As you will learn in Principle 5, Avoid the fire starters, criticism is a fire starter that often leads to feelings of disconnection with your partner
     - Backtrack and quickly apologize

   Example

   I am sorry. That sounded so critical and that's not what I meant. What I want to say instead is ... or I'm so sorry, can I start over?

   - If YOUR PARTNER becomes critical:
     - Let your partner know in the moment that what they said felt critical, ask them if they could restate their message in a softer tone

   Example

   Hey, please stop. I am feeling criticized when you talk that way and in that tone. Can you say what you want to say in a different way and in a softer tone?

Personal Insight	**Spiritual Intimacy**
	Spiritual intimacy is very important to each of us. But because Michael and I have different spiritual backgrounds, this tended to create space between us as we practiced our own spiritual rituals. So, early in our relationship, instead of praying **with** each other, we ended up praying separately **for** each other.
	At the same time, we wanted to continue to pursue deeper levels of spiritual intimacy together. As a result, we had to be intentional about:
	• Praying together
	• Meditating together
	• Reading spiritual material together
	• Listening to spiritual leaders together
	• Having spiritual discussions

Summary and Close

Let's recap what we covered in this principle.
- I started with talking about what is intimacy and what does it mean to have intimacy at deeper levels.
- Then I focused on how to assess the depth of intimacy in your relationship and the three keys for deeper intimacy.
- I identified five strategies to establish a pattern of healthy intimacy along with three strategies to employ should intimacy break down.

Intimacy is a rich concept with multiple layers and depths. However, as you learned in this principle, intimacy requires paying close attention to the 3 S's: Sharing, Seeking, and Supporting. Share your thoughts, feelings, and concerns; seek to know your partner at deeper levels; and be supportive always of your partner when they do share their intimate thoughts.

The rewards of doing so can be tremendous. For as you deepen the intimacy, you increase the richness of the relationship and strengthen the bonds that lead to your lifelong honeymoon.

<table>
<tr><td>Practicing the Principle</td><td>The Intimacy Game is a fun activity that provides a vehicle for you and your partner to increase your level of intimacy. Take the time now to play a round of the game (seven questions each). Consider playing the game monthly or quarterly to continue to get to know one another at a deeper level.</td></tr>
</table>

The Intimacy Game

Purpose

The purpose of The Intimacy Game is for you and your partner to deepen your intimacy across a variety of categories.

Directions

1. Decide who will go first.
2. The player will roll the two dice and total the number. The total indicates the category of the question as shown on the Intimacy Game Chart below.

3: The Past	**4: Stress**	**5: Love**
6: Self	**7: Relationship**	**8: Partner**
9: Sex	**10: Career/Finances**	**11: If …**
(Doubles are wild … see below)		

3. The person can choose to ask their partner any question in the category.
4. The other partner responds to the question, and then it's that partner's turn to roll the dice and ask a question.
5. Doubles are wild, so if the person rolls a double (i.e., both dice are the same number), the person chooses both the category and the question to ask.
6. The game ends after both partners have responded to seven questions.

Additional Guidelines, Recommendations, and Alternatives

Some couples have found it helpful to implement one or more of the following.

- Once a partner answers the question, the other partner has the option to ask one or two follow-up questions to gain a deeper understanding.
- Note that the questions are designed for relationships of all lengths— those that have been going for 40 years, those going for just four weeks, and everything in between. Therefore, some of the questions may not be appropriate for your relationship. Just skip those questions.
- A partner may be uncomfortable answering a question. If that is the case, the partner has the option of saying, "That question deserves further thought; let me answer a different one instead."

The goal is to deepen intimacy, not to block it. So, remember:

- **Don't ask a question you don't want the answer to!** If you feel you may be glad or sad depending upon the answer, it's likely a question you shouldn't ask at the present time.
- **Don't answer a question that you are not ready to give your thoughts and feelings about**.
- And whatever you do, **don't be dishonest** in the intimacy game. Dishonesty, long term, surely serves as a block to intimacy.

Make your own rules, add your own questions, but be sure to make it fun as you and your partner deepen your understanding of one another!

If you don't have dice, on-line dice can be found:
https://www.online-stopwatch.com/chance-games/dice-shaker-cup/

The Intimacy Game Chart

Roll doubles: Choose any section, any question.

3: The Past
1. What is your favorite childhood memory?
2. Which of your family members were you closest to growing up and why do you think that was?
3. Do you have any big regrets from your youth?
4. Were there any beliefs your parents or primary caregivers had that you grew to reject as an adult?
5. What is the most romantic thing that someone has done for you?
6. What's the worst thing that has ever happened to you?
7. Are there any past actions that might cause problems for you in the future?
8. Has there been a phase of your life that was truly bad for you?

4: Stress
1. What causes you stress or anxiety?
2. What is your biggest fear?
3. What is something that intimidates you?
4. When was the last time you cried, and why?
5. What do you believe to be unforgivable and why?
6. Of all the things you don't know how to do, which one are you the most embarrassed about?
7. What were you last really upset about, and when was that?
8. When you're upset, do you want me to try to calm you down, just listen to you, go away, or do something else?

5: Love
1. How do you know when you are in love?
2. How do you personally express your love for your partner?
3. What is romance for you?
4. What's the craziest thing that you have done for love?
5. How do you like to be complimented?
6. What is one thing that you think is unforgivable in a relationship?
7. Tell me about a time when your heart was broken.
8. What is the one relationship advice that has always stayed with you?

6: Self
1. What brings you the most joy in life?
2. What accomplishment of yours makes you most proud?
3. What is one thing you would never want to change about yourself?
4. What is that one habit that you are trying to change for a better future?
5. What is one skill you do not have that you would like to have?
6. What would you do if you won a million dollars?
7. What's the dumbest thing you've ever done?
8. With the exception of me, what are you most grateful for in life?

7: The Relationship
1. What do you think is the biggest strength in our relationship?
2. What part of our relationship makes you happiest?
3. What's your favorite memory from our relationship so far?
4. When was the time you've felt the closest to me?
5. Why do you think that we are a good match for each other?
6. What is the biggest area for improvement in our relationship?
7. What is one thing I can do to be a better partner for you?
8. If our relationship were to end, what do you think would be the likely cause?

8: Your Partner
1. What traits about me are special to you?
2. What are the three main things you think we have in common?
3. What is one deep thing you have learned from me?
4. What's a bad habit I have that bothers you?
5. What is one thing you would never want me to change about myself?
6. What activity do you most enjoy doing with me?
7. When you tell other people about me, what do you say?
8. What do you think is your most prominent shortcoming as a partner?

9: Sex	10: Career/Finances	11: IF...
1. Do you have any sexual fantasies you think about often?	1. Is there a particular dream that you have for your future?	1. If you could describe yourself in three words, what would you say?
2. Is there anything sexual we have not tried that you would like to try?	2. What do you like most about your current career?	2. If you could describe me in three words, what would you say?
3. Is there a sexual boundary that you would want your partner to respect at all times?	3. What do you like least about your current career?	3. If today were your last day to live, what would you be most proud of about your life?
4. On a 1-to-10 scale where 10 is highest, how happy are you with our sex life ... and what could bring it closer to a 10?	4. What is your ultimate career goal?	4. If today were your last day to live, how would you want to spend it?
5. What is the one thing that I do that most turns you on?	5. If you weren't doing what you are doing now, what career would you most likely have?	5. If money wasn't an issue, what expensive thing would you buy for yourself?
6. Is there anything that I do while having sex that doesn't work for you?	6. What has been your most important financial accomplishment?	6. If your house were on fire and loved ones were safe, but you had time to save one thing, what would it be?
7. What is the craziest thing you've done sexually?	7. What has been your biggest financial mistake?	7. If you could change one big decision in your life, what would it be?
8. What would make our sexual relationship better for you?	8. What are your major debts?	8. If you could change one thing about me what would it be?

Notes

Notes

Principle 3:
Lift Your Partner … Every Day

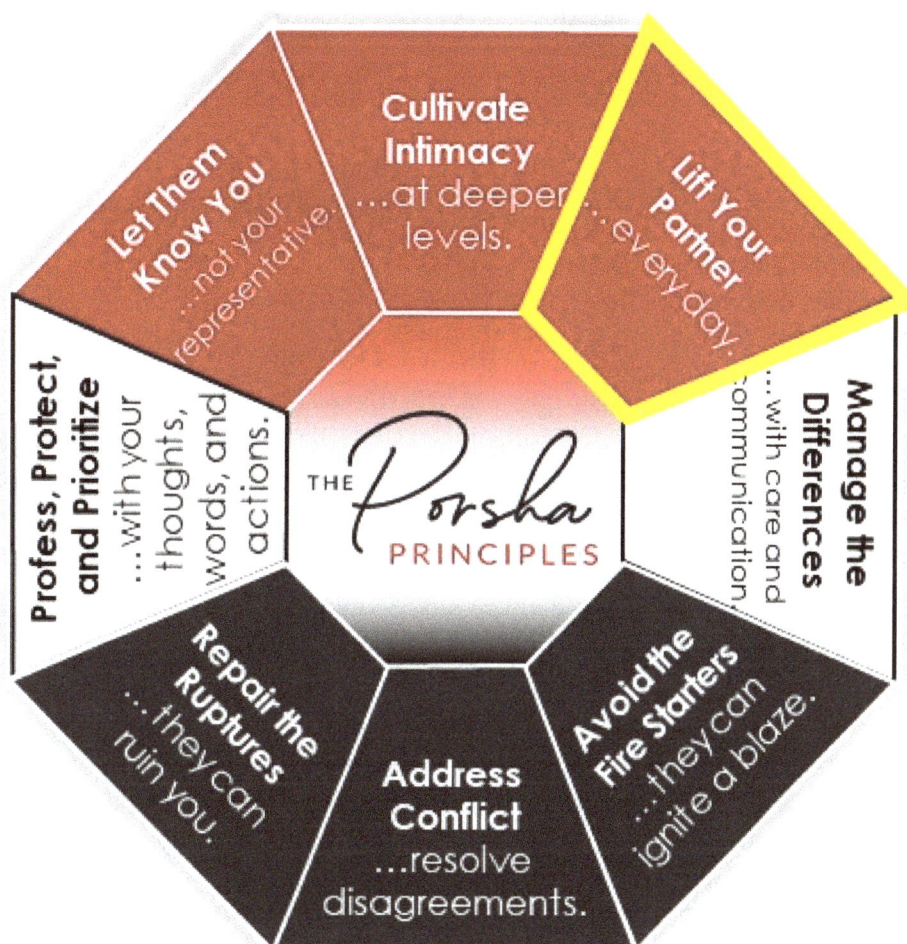

The Porsha Principles wheel with the following segments:
- **Cultivate Intimacy** …at deeper levels.
- **Lift Your Partner** …every day.
- **Let Them Know You** …not your representative.
- **Manage the Differences** …with care and communication.
- **Profess, Protect, and Prioritize** …with your thoughts, words, and actions.
- **Repair the Ruptures** …they can ruin you.
- **Address Conflict** …resolve disagreements.
- **Avoid the Fire Starters** …they can ignite a blaze.

THE *Porsha* PRINCIPLES

What You Will Learn	
	Foundation
	• What can happen if you don't pay attention to lifting your partner every day
	• The magic love language question that will reveal your partner's love language
	Proactive Strategies
	• Eight strategies for creating a habit of lifting your partner every day
	Intervention Strategies
	• What to do when you or your partner aren't feeling lifted
	Action
	• Steps you and your partner can take to put the principle into practice: "How to Love Me"

Introduction

It's been a couple of years since Pam and Marcus were married. They both have complaints about not feeling special to the other partner. Let's listen in on Pam's view.

Marcus is a good and loyal man. He is very successful and a hard worker. He often compliments me and talks about how he appreciates me for having a successful career, while also creating a beautiful home for us to live in. Even though he works late many nights, I never fear that he may be cheating on me. But I still feel emotionally neglected at times and sometimes very alone in the relationship. I can't get him to understand that despite all the good things he is doing, what I really need in order to feel loved just isn't happening with us.

It's perhaps not surprising that Marcus is also feeling less than fulfilled.

Pam is a wonderful woman and I feel lucky that she chose me to be her husband. Pam is smart, kind, beautiful, and is often a great partner. At the same time, Pam is very ambitious and always seems too busy to be a part of my world. Before we were married, she understood that my work was important too. She would accompany me to business events, talk over business problems with me, and even offer insights on how I could handle my boss and peers better. These days it seems I have to beg her to talk with me about anything. It feels like I have a roommate, not a partner who is doing her part to make our life great.

You may be wondering, "What's going on in this relationship? How did they get here so quickly? What caused the honeymoon to seemingly end?" As you will see, the issue that Pam and Marcus were having is what inevitably happens when you don't pay close attention to lifting your partner every day.

The Five Love Languages

Author Gary Chapman tells the story of being asked by someone, "What happens to love after the wedding?" As he inquired further, he learned that the questioner was someone who had been married three times and had been deeply in love each time. Yet each time, after the marriage, the seeming love and desire to be with his partner had greatly diminished. And thus the reason for the question.

This question sent Chapman on a journey that resulted in him writing his groundbreaking book, *The Five Love Languages: The Secret to a Love that Lasts*.[3] In my practice, the concepts behind the five love languages have helped many couples learn how to lift their partner every day and increase their feelings of deep intimacy.

Let's start with a brief explanation of Chapman's five love languages.

1. **Words of affirmation.** People whose primary love language is words of affirmation feel loved when their partner compliments them, praises them, or says things that uplift them. In essence, this love language says:

   Your words tell me that you admire me, and that makes me feel loved.

2. **Quality time**. Spending quality time together is the top love language for some. They view time as a highly valuable commodity, and the amount of time you spend with them reflects how you feel about them.

   Your spending time with me shows me that I matter to you, and that makes me feel loved.

3. **Receiving gifts.** For some people, when you give them a gift, they feel loved. Your thoughtfulness in picking the perfect gift tells them that you were thinking of them and that they are special to you.

   Your gifts tell me that you value me and our relationship, and that makes me feel loved.

4. **Acts of service.** Others feel loved when you do things for them. It may be the simplest of things, such as cooking a meal or taking out the trash. These acts of service communicate to the other person that you have their back.

   Your actions support me, and that makes me feel loved.

5. **Physical touch.** The last love language is physical touch. Some think physical touch equals sex, but physical touch is certainly more inclusive. It includes the desire for physical closeness, caresses, strokes, hugs, and yes, sex.

   When you touch me, it shows me that you want to please me, and that makes me feel loved.

> **Our tendency is to love people the way we want to be loved. Instead, we must learn to love our partner the way they want to be loved.**

While understanding the five love languages is important, Chapman makes two other major points that are perhaps even more important for every couple to understand:

- Our tendency is to love people the way we want to be loved.

---

[3] Gary Chapman, *The Five Love Languages: The Secret to a Love that Lasts* (Chicago: Northfield Publishing, 2000).

- Instead, for our relationships to be healthy and longstanding, we must learn to love our partner the way they want to be loved.

What does this mean? If your love language is words of affirmation, your tendency will be to give words of affirmation to show your love for your partner. If your love language is giving gifts, you will tend to give gifts to show your partner love. Unfortunately, if your partner has a different love language from yours, your efforts will have little impact on contributing to the love pool.

How Do You Learn Your Partner's Love Language?

- **The Online Test.** Chapman has created an online test that you and your partner can take (https://www.5lovelanguages.com/quizzes/love-language) to discover your individual love languages. The test provides you with a list of scores which allow you to identify your top love language, as well as your second, third, fourth, and fifth in order.

- **The Magic Love Language Question**. There is a shortcut method you might find helpful, especially if your partner is reluctant to take a test. Ask your partner what I call the magic love language question: "What's the one thing I could do that would make you feel more loved by me?"

Listen closely to your partner's answer. This can often reveal your partner's love language. Let's look back at Pam and Marcus and listen closely for their love language as you hear their responses to the magic love language question.

Marcus asked: *What's the one thing I could do that would make you feel more loved by me?*

Pam's Response:

I need you to be with me more and for us to do more things together. I would love to try a new restaurant in the city every other Friday so we can talk and laugh and eat good food

From Pam's response, it is quite evident her primary love language is quality time, and this has been missing for her.

Pam asked: *What's the one thing I could do that would make you feel more loved by me?*

Marcus' Response:

I need to know you have my back. I would love it if you would commit to accompanying me to one of my business events per quarter. When you are with me in these events, it makes me feel complete: we are conquering the world together.

From Marcus' response, it is quite evident that his primary love language is acts of service and this has been missing for him.

The Power of Thinking

When I talk with any couple whose relationship is in jeopardy, either one or both of them have been thinking for quite some time about separating, having an affair, or ending the relationship. They certainly haven't been thinking about lifting their partner every day.

See, people often don't recognize their feelings and behaviors are directly influenced by their **thoughts**. If your thoughts about your partner are predominately negative, it can begin turning the "heart" you have for your partner from a glowing red to a bleak and dark black. If this continues for an extended period, you can imagine the impact it will have on your feelings and behavior toward your partner. If you want to change your behavior and feelings toward your partner, you have to start by changing your thinking. This change in thinking will then be reflected in your words, your actions, and eventually your feelings toward your partner. Maintaining positive thoughts about your partner all the time is a key to keeping those loving feelings high and keeping those sparks flying continuously.

> **Key: Maintaining positive thoughts about your partner is key to keeping those sparks flying continuously.**

Proactive Strategies

Of course, if you and your partner have similar love languages, that can make it much easier to feel loved by one another. That is, you will likely find that your partner naturally does the things you need to feel loved, because that is the way they want to be loved too.

But what if you and your partner have different primary love languages? Can the relationship still work? Of course it can. In fact, in my practice I have found that most couples have different love languages. Deep healing can come when they learn to love their partner in the way that makes their partner feel loved.

However, to do this successfully and consistently, it takes being intentional and putting in the effort. I recommend that you and your partner consider these key strategies for lifting each other every day.

1. **Start with your own thinking.**

    If you are not feeling the desire to love your partner in the way they want to be loved, or if you are feeling that the sparks seem to be dying out, start with your own thinking.

    - Nurture your fondness and admiration for your partner by such activities as:
        - Regularly reminding yourself of your partner's most positive qualities
        - Saving memories, such as pictures, letters, and other items
        - Seeking to focus on positive aspects of your partner anytime you find yourself thinking negatively about them
    - Pay close attention to how you are thinking about your partner throughout the day. When you catch yourself focused on a negative, take a minute to nurture fondness and admiration for your partner as described above.

2. **Cultivate in yourself the desire to fulfill your partner's needs.**

    Most of us are wired to look out for self first and to focus on ensuring our own needs are met. So how do you get yourself to focus on fulfilling your partner's needs?

    - Remind yourself that you love your partner and that they are the most important person in the world to you, and that contributing to their happiness is one of your highest priorities.
    - Visualize yourself taking an action that brings joy to your partner and feel the joy inside yourself when you visualize the joy on their face.

3. **Learn your partner's love language.**

    Use the love language test (https://www.5lovelanguages.com/quizzes/love-language) or the magic love language question to learn your partner's love language.

4. **Identify your own internal barriers.**

   Identify any barriers in you that may hinder your expressing love in your partner's love language. Don't be surprised if you find yourself reluctant, challenged, judgmental, or even resentful about having to adjust your actions to meet your partner's love language. Examples:

   - For a partner who did not grow up with affection through physical touch, they may feel challenged by meeting the physical touch needs of their partner because it may feel awkward to them, or they may just not be used to it.

   - A person who has gifts as their primary love language may be judged as materialistic by their partner whose primary love language is touch or acts of service.

   - Gender-specific beliefs can also be barriers. For example, a woman may feel her partner is "weak" if he needs words of affirmation to feel loved. Likewise, a man whose partner needs acts of service to feel loved may feel it's not a "manly" thing to do to help out with "woman's" work around the house.

   To overcome barriers such as these, it is always important to go back to key strategy #1: Remember you love your partner, and you want your partner to feel loved. I will discuss in Principle 4, Managing the differences, things you can do to address these barriers to lifting your partner, including dispelling negative beliefs, removing judgment and criticism, and becoming more open to loving your partner differently.

5. **Learn multiple ways to express your love in your partner's love language.**

   Knowing your partner's love language is not enough. It is essential to your lifelong honeymoon that you lift your partner every day by learning to love them the way they want to be loved. It's the small, daily acts of thoughtfulness and attention that breed intimacy and friendship. However, this can be challenging if their love language is different from yours. So, what are strategies you might use? Here are just a few strategies for showing love to your partner.

   - Words of affirmation
     - Keep a running list (mental or physical) of all the positive things your partner does, so you have them ready for use!
     - Daily leave little complimentary notes for your partner.
     - Vocalize positive thoughts and feelings about your partner in their presence and in the presence of others.
     - Write love letters or poems to your partner about how special they are to you.
   - Acts of service
     - Give your partner a day off their chores and you fill in!
     - When you see your partner has a need, don't wait until they ask for help; instead initiate helping them.
     - Ask your partner to create a list of things that they would love for you to do.

- Pay someone to come in and finish a project of your partner's choosing.
- Receiving Gifts
  - Gift your partner with their favorite things often. For example, if they like flowers, maybe subscribe to a flower club so your partner will receive this gift like clockwork!
  - Keep a notebook about the little things that your partner makes comments on; they can make perfect gifts!
  - Get creative and give your partner a coupon book full of gifts (e.g., electronic device, necklace, pair of shoes) that they can redeem whenever they like.
  - Instead of a coupon book of gifts, make the coupons various personal actions such as "good for an evening out," "good for a foot massage," or "good for taking care of a chore."
- Quality time
  - Discuss the top five things you like to do as a couple and make regular plans to do them together.
  - Surprise your partner with a babysitter and take them out for a kid-free night on the town.
  - Carve out daily "sacred space" for 30 minutes to give your partner your undivided attention.
  - Plan a surprise lunch date.
- Physical touch
  - Greet your partner with hugs and kisses regularly.
  - Let your partner know you desire them with a sexual touch.
  - At random times when you are together reach out and stroke/caress your partner.
  - Plan a sexy evening for your partner.

Be creative with your approach to your partner's love language, but everything in moderation. Avoid using the same approach every time. For example, If your partner likes physical touch, don't touch them the same way every time. Strive to be creative!

6. **Don't major in the minors.**
   - Recognize that for most of us, the tendency is to focus on loving our partner the way we want to be loved. I call that majoring in the minors because these things might not be important to your partner at all.
   - Instead, major in the majors by focusing on the things important to your partner, not the things you think should be important to them.

7. **Seek feedback from you partner on how much your actions make them feel loved.**
   - Consider doing a modified version of what Gary Chapman calls "The Tank Check." Check weekly or monthly with your partner and ask, "On a scale of 1-to-10, how much have you been feeling loved by me over

this past week?" If your partner's tank is below a 7 or 8, ask, "What can I do right now to begin refilling your tank?" While this may sound unromantic or artificial, feedback is critical to creating your lifelong honeymoon. You don't want to have long periods lacking fulfillment, which drain your love pool.

8. **Do a self-check.**

   - Adapting to another person's style is not always easy or comfortable. Therefore, it's important to be emotionally honest with yourself as you practice loving your partner in their love language. From time to time, do a self-check on how this is feeling for you. Ask yourself:
     - How does it make me feel when I am loving my partner in their love language?
     - Do I like the feeling? Why or why not?
     - If you don't like the feeling, talk about your discomfort with your partner and the things you both can do to support you.

Intervention Strategies

What should you do when YOU are not feeling loved?

Find a time to give your partner feedback. If it feels too hard to say it, write a letter to your partner. Below is a helpful approach for you to consider.

1. Start with positivity.

   I know you love me and that my feeling loved is important to you.

2. State your intention by sharing how you are feeling and how important it is to you to bring about a change.

   I know that over the past several weeks I haven't felt that love from you, and I want to see what we can do to address that.

3. Make your request.

   You know that my primary love language is quality time, and I have been really missing it and missing you. One of the things I think can help is if we can make it a priority to have dinner together at least five times each week. That way I will know that I will get quality time with you regularly.

   Can you make sure you are home by 6:00 pm on the nights that we commit to eat dinner together?

4. Get input.

   How do you feel about this suggestion?

5. Seek alternatives if necessary.

   Do you have a different suggestion?

6. Confirm agreement.

   So, we are in agreement then that we will...

7. Have a monitoring process.

Interventions often are needed to correct an unhelpful pattern. But, without a monitoring process, the unhelpful pattern can set in again. Therefore, have a periodic check-in process to ensure that you continue to love one another the way each of you needs to be loved.

What do you do when YOUR PARTNER tells you they are not feeling loved by you?

1. Let them know you heard them by restating their message.
   Let me make sure I got this right. What I hear you saying is …

2. Validate what you can by giving points when you can see why they may be feeling that way.
   I can see your point because I have been …

3. Be emotionally responsive by joining with them in how they are feeling, comforting them, and seeking to understand more.
   I am sorry that you are been feeling this way. It is really important to me that I contribute to you feeling loved …

4. Stay open to making changes and repair.
   Would it help if I…. What other things might help?

5. Come to agreement on an approach.
   So, we are in agreement then that we will …

6. Have a monitoring process.

Deeper Dive

When we enter this world as babies, it is natural that we focus on our needs and not the needs of others. As we grow up, we often learn to move from being self-centered to more others-centered, many times because it is in our enlightened self-interest. At the same time, we may find it difficult to practice focusing on lifting others when we are faced with daily life stressors (e.g., paying bills, work deadlines, the needs of children).

Though lifting your partner every day is a healthy and loving thing to do, it may not come naturally for many people, based on their own history and experiences. Whether it is easy for you or difficult, you may find these questions helpful in digging deeper to understand why this is so.

- What did you see your parents or primary caregivers do to lift each other up?
- In what ways did others around you love one another?
- When you were loved by someone important to you in your love language, how did that make you feel? How did you respond to that person?
- When someone important to you didn't love you in your love language, how did that make you feel? How did you respond to that person?

From your answers to these questions, and given your past experiences, do you notice any similarities or differences in how you feel and act when lifting your current partner up?

Summary and Close

To live your lifelong honeymoon, lifting your partner every day is fundamental. Unfortunately, this is one of the most forgotten principles. As you learned in this principle, to lift your partner every day, you must:

- Use the power of thinking to influence your feelings about your partner and your actions toward them
- Cultivate in yourself the desire to fulfill your partner's needs
- Learn your partner's love language
- Identify your own internal barriers
- Learn multiple ways to express your love in your partner's love language.
- Don't major in the minors
- Seek feedback from you partner on how much your actions make them feel loved
- Do a self-check on how adapting to your partner's love language is working for you

> **Understanding your partner's love language and committing to take the actions to love them the way they want to be loved is a critical piece in creating and sustaining your lifelong honeymoon.**

Once you master your partner's love language and commit to practicing it daily, you are surely on your way to living your lifelong honeymoon.

Practicing the Principle	**How to Love Me**
	Understanding your partner's love language and committing to take the actions to love them the way they want to be loved is a critical piece to creating and sustaining your lifelong honeymoon.
	Take the following steps to put Principle 3 into practice.
	1. Have you and your partner take the love language assessment if you haven't already done so.
	2. Do the Tank Check exercise by taking turns asking the following questions of each other.
	• What are things that I have done in the last seven days that have contributed to you feeling loved?
	• On a scale of 1-to-10 with 10 being high, how filled is your love tank right now?
	• What are two or three things I could do over the next week to help move you closer to a 10?
	3. Repeat the Tank Check exercise every week for four to eight weeks, to help make paying attention to your partner's love language a nearly unconscious habit.

Notes

Principle 4:
Manage the Differences ... with Care and Communication

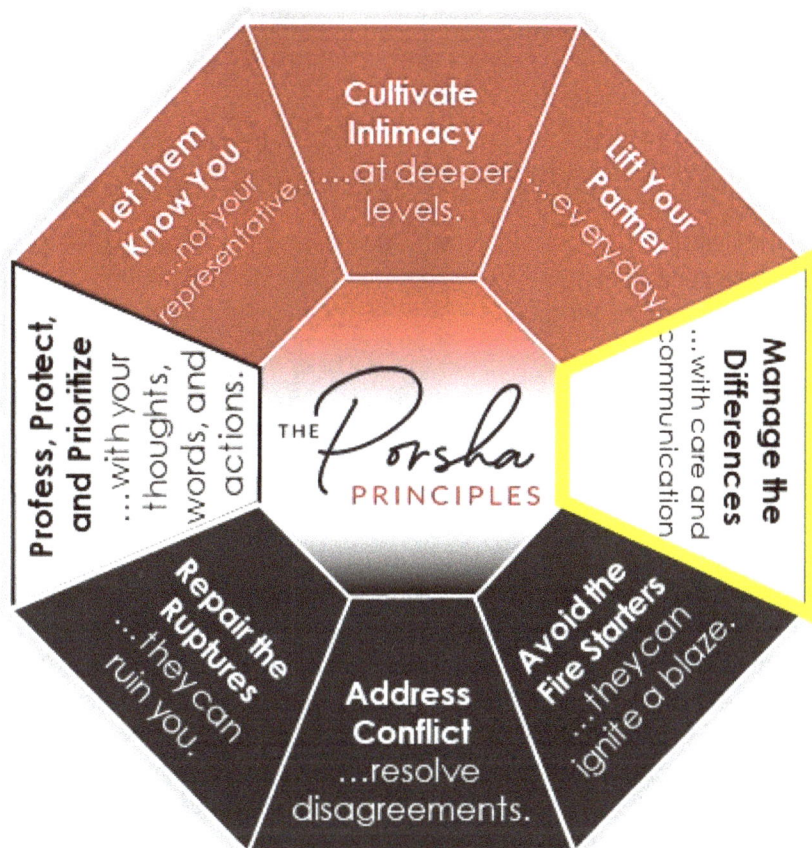

The Porsha Principles

- Cultivate Intimacy ...at deeper levels.
- Lift Your Partner ...every day.
- Manage the Differences ...with care and communication
- Avoid the Fire Starters ...they can ignite a blaze.
- Address Conflict ...resolve disagreements.
- Repair the Ruptures ...they can ruin you.
- Profess, Protect, and Prioritize ...with your thoughts, words, and actions.
- Let Them Know You ...not your representative

What You Will Learn	
	Foundation
	• Why is it important to manage the differences?
	• How to use the DISC model to understand basic personality differences
	• How to use the Style Comparison Table to identify likely differences
	Proactive Strategies
	• Proactive strategies for managing the differences
	Intervention Strategies
	• How to recover when you or your partner have mismanaged a difference
	Action
	• Steps you and your partner can take to put the principle into practice: "The Couples Tendency Profile"

Introduction

When two people come together, they bring with them different ways of seeing things and different ways of doing things. These differences often cause friction in the relationship. And if not handled well, they can lead to major disruptions and sometimes ruptures in the relationship. One of the keys to creating your lifelong honeymoon is being able to manage these differences well.

Let's listen to Marcus and Pam as they describe differences that showed up early in their relationship. We'll start with a difference that Marcus experienced.

I can remember the first time we were choosing where to go eat. I remember saying, "We've been shopping this whole afternoon. It's close to six o'clock. Let's choose a restaurant quickly to go to. What do you think about …" and I mentioned a popular seafood restaurant. Pam's response was, "No I'm not in the mood for seafood." I said, "Okay, what about Italian?" Pam's response: "No, I am not feeling that either." Although I was hungry, I tried to stay patient and asked her, "Okay, what are you feeling?" Pam then pulls out her phone to search the Internet for alternatives. Twenty minutes later, she chooses a place. I was starving and very irritable.

Clearly Marcus was ready to make a decision quickly, and Pam needed more time. Though this is a single example, this difference in the way they make decisions was a source of friction in other areas of their relationships as well. As in this situation, Marcus generally makes decision very quickly with minimal information. Pam's natural decision-making style is much more deliberate and thoughtful and requires more time. This difference can often be a benefit to them as a couple, but not when one of them is starving and irritable! In this case, they mismanaged that difference.

Let's hear from Pam about a difference that was significant for her early in their relationship.

It's pool day, and I am looking forward to Marcus and I spending quiet quality time at the pool together. But as soon as we walk through the gate of the pool, Marcus sees several other people at the pool and shouts to them, "Great weather for a pool day!" He starts conversing with them, and it's like he forgot that this was our time, not time to be social with others. I grabbed his hand to try to pull him away to find a private place for us. But he doesn't read my signal and keeps speaking to the other people. I just walk away, find a place, and sit down, alone.

While the prior example highlighted a decision-making difference, this example highlights a difference in social interaction. Marcus clearly prefers considerable social interaction with groups, while Pam generally prefers social interactions with those close to her.

There are many models that help people understand differences in personality style, thinking style, communication style, etc., including such assessment tools as the Meyers-Briggs Type Indicators, the Herrmann Brain Dominance Indicator, and the Enneagram. In my work, I like the simplicity of the DISC model as a tool for helping couples understand and manage their differences.

Let's start with a basic understanding of the four styles, courtesy of my husband's book, *Buying Styles – Selling the Way Your Customer Buys*[4].

---

[4] Michael Wilkinson, *Buying Styles – Selling the Way Your Customer Buys* (New York: Amacomm, 2009).

Understanding the Styles

The High-D Style

In the DISC model, "D" stands for drive or dominance. Imagine that there is a wall in front of us, and the objective is to get to the other side of the wall. High-Ds lower their shoulders, get a running start, and break through the wall. High-Ds get things done. They take a direct, assertive approach to solving problems. They enjoy challenges and get satisfaction from overcoming them.

When you think of high-Ds, think of CEOs, entrepreneurs, directors, school principals, and team leaders. What's the key value high-Ds bring to relationships? You probably have already figured it out. High-Ds focus their efforts on getting things done, they address problems directly, and they make tough decisions quickly. Unfortunately, they also have a downside.

You know when you are in the presence of a high-D. They are always pushing. They always want to win—no matter the cost. They also tend to be so concerned about the goal that they don't consider the impact on you or others. And they tend to make decisions too quickly before having all the facts.

Why do they do this? Because of their *key factor—time*. When you think of high-Ds, think "time." Don't waste their time. They have too much to do. So how do you communicate with a high-D? Well, think of it this way.

High-D Key Factor: Time	
Communication Do's	Communication Don'ts
1. Be prepared—get to the point rather quickly	1. Don't waste their time with idle chatter
2. State your points clearly, *briefly*, specifically	2. Don't ramble or tell long stories
3. Give only as much detail as necessary; let them control	3. Don't be too detailed unless they ask for it

To summarize, you can remember how to interact with your high-D partner by keeping in mind the following key phrase for high-Ds.

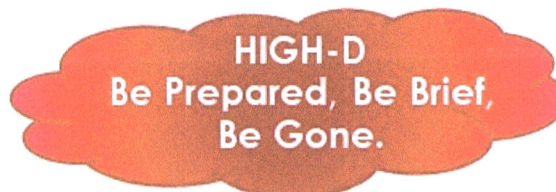

**HIGH-D
Be Prepared, Be Brief,
Be Gone.**

The High-I Style

I've talked about the high-D. Let's move on to the second style in the DISC model. "I" stands for influence. High-Is enjoy helping people see the big picture. They motivate and inspire others to succeed. While high-Ds break through the wall, high-Is motivate people over the wall. They are the ones with the megaphone yelling, "Hey everyone. We have a wall to get over. Come on. It will be great on the other side. We can do it. Go Team! Go Team! Over the Wall!"

When you think of high-Is, think of salespeople, teachers, and facilitators. What are the strengths high-Is bring to the relationship? High-Is are able to see the big picture. They are great at motivating and selling their ideas to others. They create a dynamic environment that is almost always fun. They like relationships and working with people. They are also highly creative.

But, like the high-Ds, high-Is also have a downside. They can be so talkative that they don't listen. They can also spend so much time on the vision that they never execute. And, because they focus on ideas, they tend to overlook details. Why do they do this? Because of their *key factor: being heard*. High-Is like the stage. They enjoy having an audience with whom to interact.

So how do you communicate with a high-I? Take a look at the following chart.

High-I Key Factor: Being Heard	
Communication Do's	Communication Don'ts
1. Give them the big picture before going into details	1. Don't dwell on details and facts; provide them in writing instead
2. Give them a chance to share their ideas	2. Don't tell them what to do without giving them an opportunity to respond
3. Keep the conversation friendly and warm	3. Don't allow them to ramble too long

If your partner is a high-I, you can remember how to interact with them by keeping in mind this key phrase.

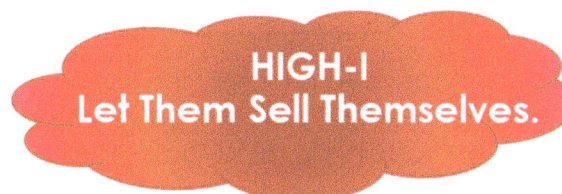

**HIGH-I
Let Them Sell Themselves.**

See, if *you* are trying to sell to a high-I, the wrong person is speaking! If you want to sell high-Is, you have to get *them* talking about *your* idea. Ask them what they need in a solution. Ask them to describe how it would work. Then, after outlining your idea, ask them to talk about the benefits. Remember, you have to let them sell themselves.

The High-S Style

"S" stands for steadiness. High-Ss tend to be the stabilizing force in a relationship. They tend to be dependable and loyal, and prefer a stable, secure environment. They love to help. While the high-Ds are busting through the wall and the high-Is are cheering people on, the high-Ss are quietly at the wall lending people a hand, helping people over it. For the person needing a boost, the high-Ss will supply it. For those needing a lift, the high-S will crouch down, link hands, and provide the lift.

What are the classic occupations for High Ss? Social service workers, civil servants, retail clerks. What are the strengths the high-Ss bring to the relationship? High-Ss tend to be supportive and dependable. They are people-oriented and good listeners. They are accommodating and tolerant of others.

Unfortunately, they also have a downside. High-Ss often avoid dealing with issues until they become big problems. This happens because they really dislike confrontation. So, if you do something that upsets a high-S, they will likely take it again and again, until one day they explode. Many of us might think, "I don't understand, all I did was …" but what we don't see are all the things that have been building up. So, one downside of high-Ss is that they don't like confrontation. Another is that they can be slow to accept change, and they hold grudges. And finally, they can appear to lack vision and creativity. That's because they are trying to make things work while ensuring that everyone is comfortable.

One of the reasons high-Ss dislike confrontation is because of their **key factor: being liked.** High-Ss want to be liked. They want harmony. They want everyone to get along. So how do you communicate with a high-S?

High-S Key Factor: Being Liked	
Communication Do's	Communication Don'ts
1. Start with a personal comment	1. Don't dive straight into business
2. Present ideas deliberately and clearly; provide assurances	2. Don't be demanding or abrasive
3. Make sure they are in agreement before moving on	3. Don't assume silence means consent

If you are demanding and abrasive to a high-S, the high-S will shut down, and so you can't assume that silence means consent. You can remember how to communicate with high-Ss by keeping in mind the following key phrase.

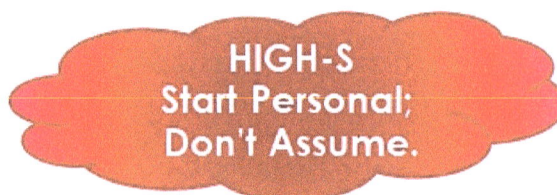

**HIGH-S
Start Personal;
Don't Assume.**

The High-C Style

"C" stands for Compliance. High-Cs tend to rely on rational logic and evidence to reach conclusions. They make sure that things are done by the book.

To get over the wall, the high-Cs would do their measurement, determine exactly where they have to stand, how high they would have to leap, and what force would be needed to clear the wall. In addition they would want to walk you through each calculation. When you think of typical occupations for high-Cs, think of researchers, accountants, engineers, analysts, and other detailed or quantitative professions. What are the strengths that high-Cs bring to a relationship? High-Cs tend to be organized and detail-oriented. They make sure that decisions are well supported by facts and figures. It's the high-Cs who help ensure that we think things through before making a decision.

Unfortunately, like all the other styles, high-Cs also have a downside. High-Cs can be perfectionists and very hard to please. Not only do they have high expectations for themselves, they tend to also have high expectations for those around them. High-Cs can also be so focused on facts and figures that they ignore the people side, resulting in their sometimes being considered cold and calculating. Finally, high-Cs can be overly cautious and suffer from analysis paralysis—taking far too long to make even the smallest of decisions.

Why do they do this? Because of their *key factor: getting it right*. High-Cs want to get it right. They would rather make no decision at all then to make the wrong decision.

So how do you communicate with a high-C? You basically have to build a logical case that makes it obvious to them that they are making the right decision.

High-C Key Factor: Getting It Right	
Communication Do's	Communication Don'ts
1. Present ideas in a logical fashion 2. Stay on topic 3. Provide facts and figures that back up claims	1. Don't be disorganized or make random comments 2. Don't rely on emotional appeals to gain agreement 3. Don't force a rapid decision

To summarize, you can remember how to communicate with your high-C partner by keeping in mind this key phrase for high-Cs:

**HIGH C
Give Them Time
for the Details.**

Understanding the Differences

So, we've talked about the four basic DISC styles, now let's focus on the differences that frequently show up between them. We'll do this by examining behaviors across two-dimensions: direct vs. indirect and task-oriented vs. people-oriented, as illustrated by the graphic that follows.

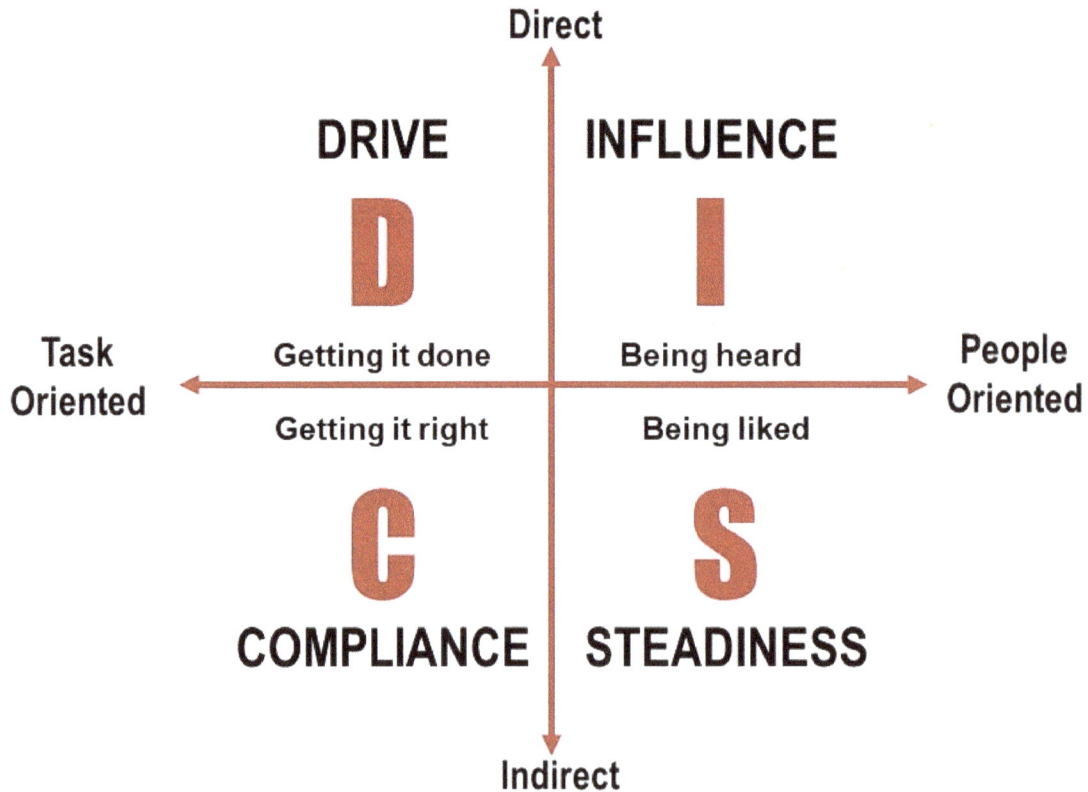

Direct vs. Indirect

The graphic that follows shows that high-Ds and high-Is tend to be direct in their approach, while high-Ss and high-Cs tend to be indirect.

Direct (High-Ds / High-Is)	vs.	Indirect (High-Ss / High-Cs)
Decisive	vs.	Deliberate
Proactive	vs.	Reactive
Risk-taking	vs.	Risk-avoiding
Conflict-resolving	vs.	Conflict-avoiding

Task-Oriented vs. People Oriented

But when it comes to task versus people orientation, high-Ds and high-Cs match up as task-oriented, and high-Is and high-Ss match up as people-oriented.

Task-Oriented (High-Ds / High-Cs)	vs.	People-Oriented (High-Is / High-Ss)
Objective	vs.	Subjective
Outcome-focused	vs.	Relationship-focused
Questioning	vs.	Accepting
Time scheduled	vs.	Time flexible

Introduction to the Style Comparison Tables

We can now use these dimensions to compare how the styles match up as a couple and identify where differences are likely to occur in a relationship. Of course, couples that share the same style naturally match up in all areas. However, this doesn't mean that they don't have issues. It only means that their approach to solving them will likely be similar. However, the downside to each style described earlier would likely be magnified, as you will see.

The ten Style Comparison Tables appear in the Appendix. Each table compares a unique DISC combination, starting with a couple where both partners have high-D as their dominant style (D | D), followed by a couple where one is a high-D and the other a high-I (D | I), and then the D | S table and so on. Shaded areas in each table represent areas of similarity between the styles.

You can use the tables to gain a broad overview of areas where you and your partner may have differences in style that impact your relationship. Some differences you may experience as minor. Others may significantly impact your relationship. I have included the first three tables here for comparison.

Table 1: High-D / High-D	D	D
• If both partners are high-Ds, they will likely both share characteristics such as decisiveness, being proactive, risk-taking, and being outcome-focused. • However, while they will likely accomplish a lot as a couple, they might have problems with each one making decisions on their own without collaboration or taking the needs of the other into account.	Decisive	
	Proactive	
	Risk-taking	
	Conflict-resolving	
	Objective	
	Outcome-focused	
	Questioning	
	Time scheduled	

Table 2: High-D / High-I

- As you can see, they are similar in the gray areas: decisive, proactive, risk-taking, and conflict-resolving.
- However, they differ in the four other areas. These differences, if not managed well, could lead to significant abrasions in the relationship.
- In particular, with the high-D focused on outcomes, and the high-I focused on relationships, they might have considerable issues when a decision has to been made that includes trade-offs between achieving a desired result and negatively impacting others.

D	I
Decisive	
Proactive	
Risk-taking	
Conflict-resolving	
Objective	Subjective
Outcome-focused	Relationship-focused
Questioning	Accepting
Time scheduled	Time flexible

Table 3: High-D / High-S

- The high-D / high-S is one of the two couple combinations that can be highly complementary or highly conflicting depending upon whether the two people can respect and honor the differences.
- These two styles are different on every one of the dimensions, and this can lead to high levels of conflict in a variety of areas.
- However, if they can value the different perspectives, they can leverage the differences in a highly positive way. As an example, in terms of decision-making, if they recognize that the high-D is able to be decisive and the high-S deliberate, they can use the strength of one or the other depending upon what type of decision is needed in a given situation.

D	S
Decisive	Deliberate
Proactive	Reactive
Risk-taking	Risk-avoiding
Conflict-resolving	Conflict-avoiding
Objective	Subjective
Outcome-focused	Relationship-focused
Questioning	Accepting
Time scheduled	Time flexible

Refer to Appendix I to see all ten Style Comparison Tables.

Focusing on Your Key Differences

The Style Comparison Tables can help you identify differences based on your DISC type. However, to further focus on identifying your key differences, I recommend you and your partner complete my **Couples Tendency Profile**.

The Couples Tendency Profile is a tool for helping you and your partner identify areas where you are different and where you are similar. The first eight dimensions correspond to the eight sub-dimensions used in the Style Comparison Tables. The last twelve dimensions represent the other most common areas that I have seen couples struggle with.

Couples Tendency Profile

How to Complete the Profile

- Print out two copies of the profile for you and your partner to complete separately. It can be helpful for each of you to use a different colored marker.
- **Important:** With each question, first choose if you are on the left side **(L)** or the right side **(R)**.
- Next, circle 1, 2, or 3 to indicate how strong your tendency is for that side.
- Once you have both completed the profile, come together, switch markers, and share your answers and place your partner's answer on your profile. This way you will each have the completed profile with both partner's answers circled in the different marker colors.

Keep in Mind

At different times and under different circumstances, most of us can be on one end of the spectrum, while other times at the other end. Therefore, in completing the profile, respond based on what you **generally** tend to do in **most** situations.

---

1. DECISIONS

DECISIVE. I tend to make decisions quickly.

DELIBERATE. I tend to give due consideration before making a decision.

Strong Tendency	Moderate Tendency	Slight Tendency		Slight Tendency	Moderate Tendency	Strong Tendency
L3	L2	L1	0	R1	R2	R3

---

2. ACTION

PROACTIVE. I tend to take action in anticipation of what might happen.

REACTIVE. I tend to address situations as they occur.

Strong Tendency	Moderate Tendency	Slight Tendency		Slight Tendency	Moderate Tendency	Strong Tendency
L3	L2	L1	0	R1	R2	R3

---

3. RISK

RISK-TAKING. I tend to take risks if the potential reward is worth it.

RISK-AVOIDING. I tend to avoid risk unless the potential negative impact is minimal.

Strong Tendency	Moderate Tendency	Slight Tendency		Slight Tendency	Moderate Tendency	Strong Tendency
L3	L2	L1	0	R1	R2	R3

---

4. CONFLICT

CONFLICT-RESOLVING. I tend to try to quickly resolve conflict when a conflict appears.

CONFLICT-TOLERANT. I tend to be tolerant of conflict until it becomes necessary to address.

Strong Tendency	Moderate Tendency	Slight Tendency		Slight Tendency	Moderate Tendency	Strong Tendency
L3	L2	L1	0	R1	R2	R3

5. EVALUATION

OBJECTIVE. I tend to focus more on objective data in my decisions.

SUBJECTIVE. I tend to focus more on subjective information in my decisions.

Strong Tendency	Moderate Tendency	Slight Tendency		Slight Tendency	Moderate Tendency	Strong Tendency
L3	L2	L1	0	R1	R2	R3

6. FOCUS

OUTCOME-FOCUSED. I tend to focus on ensuring outcomes are achieved.

RELATIONSHIP-FOCUSED. I tend to focus on ensuring people are taken care of.

Strong Tendency	Moderate Tendency	Slight Tendency		Slight Tendency	Moderate Tendency	Strong Tendency
L3	L2	L1	0	R1	R2	R3

7. RECEPTIVITY

QUESTIONING. I tend to question others' ideas when presented to me.

RECEPTIVE. I tend to be receptive of others' ideas when presented to me.

Strong Tendency	Moderate Tendency	Slight Tendency		Slight Tendency	Moderate Tendency	Strong Tendency
L3	L2	L1	0	R1	R2	R3

8. TIME

TIME SCHEDULED. I tend to schedule most of my activities.

TIME FLEXIBLE. I tend to keep my schedule flexible and limit scheduled activities

Strong Tendency	Moderate Tendency	Slight Tendency		Slight Tendency	Moderate Tendency	Strong Tendency
L3	L2	L1	0	R1	R2	R3

9. FINANCES

SPENDER. I tend to put a higher priority on spending money to acquire what I want.

SAVER. I tend to put a higher priority on saving money and building wealth.

Strong Tendency	Moderate Tendency	Slight Tendency		Slight Tendency	Moderate Tendency	Strong Tendency
L3	L2	L1	0	R1	R2	R3

10. SEXUAL ACTIVITY

HIGH LIBIDO. I tend to have a high libido and prefer to engage in frequent sexual activity.

LOW LIBIDO. I tend to have a low libido and prefer to engage in less sexual activity.

Strong Tendency	Moderate Tendency	Slight Tendency		Slight Tendency	Moderate Tendency	Strong Tendency
L3	L2	L1	0	R1	R2	R3

11. PARENTING

STRICT. I tend to parent with strict rules and less flexibility.

FLEXIBLE. I tend to parent with flexibility and less strict rules.

Strong Tendency	Moderate Tendency	Slight Tendency		Slight Tendency	Moderate Tendency	Strong Tendency
L3	L2	L1	0	R1	R2	R3

12. FAMILY FOCUS

HIGH FAMILY FOCUS. I tend to put a higher value on spending time with family.

LOW FAMILY FOCUS. I tend to put a lower value on spending time with family.

Strong Tendency	Moderate Tendency	Slight Tendency		Slight Tendency	Moderate Tendency	Strong Tendency
L3	L2	L1	0	R1	R2	R3

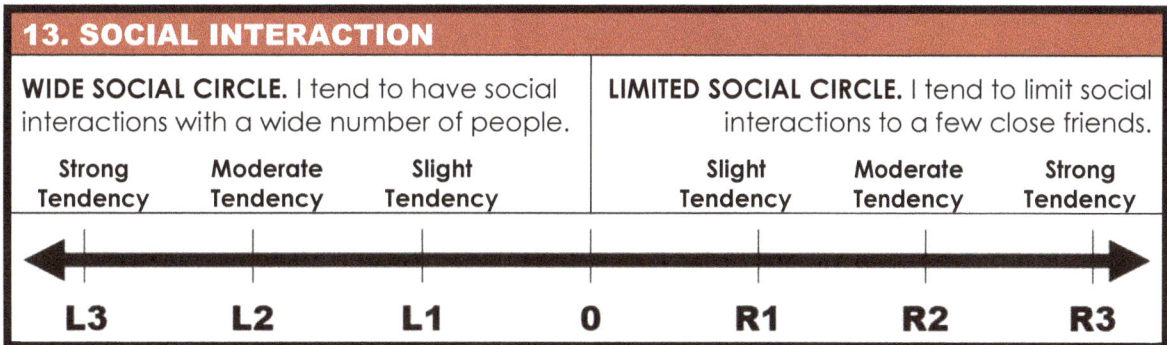

13. SOCIAL INTERACTION

WIDE SOCIAL CIRCLE. I tend to have social interactions with a wide number of people.

LIMITED SOCIAL CIRCLE. I tend to limit social interactions to a few close friends.

Strong Tendency	Moderate Tendency	Slight Tendency		Slight Tendency	Moderate Tendency	Strong Tendency
L3	L2	L1	0	R1	R2	R3

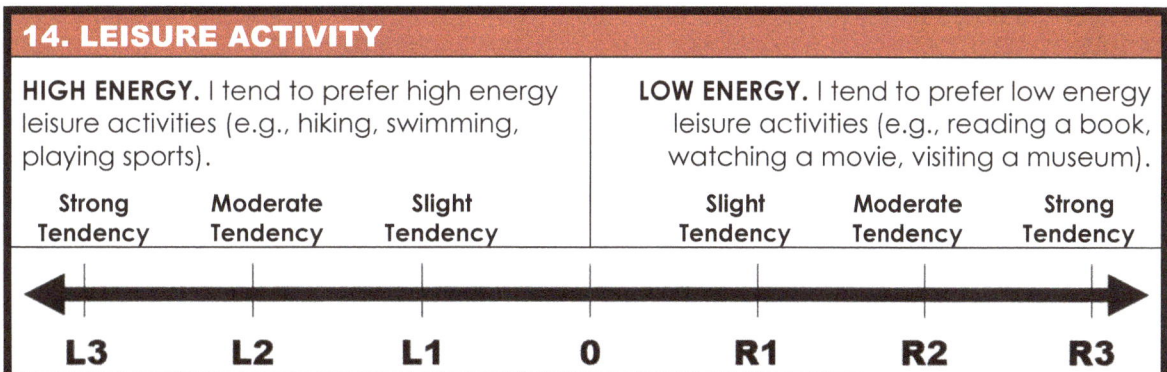

14. LEISURE ACTIVITY

HIGH ENERGY. I tend to prefer high energy leisure activities (e.g., hiking, swimming, playing sports).

LOW ENERGY. I tend to prefer low energy leisure activities (e.g., reading a book, watching a movie, visiting a museum).

Strong Tendency	Moderate Tendency	Slight Tendency		Slight Tendency	Moderate Tendency	Strong Tendency
L3	L2	L1	0	R1	R2	R3

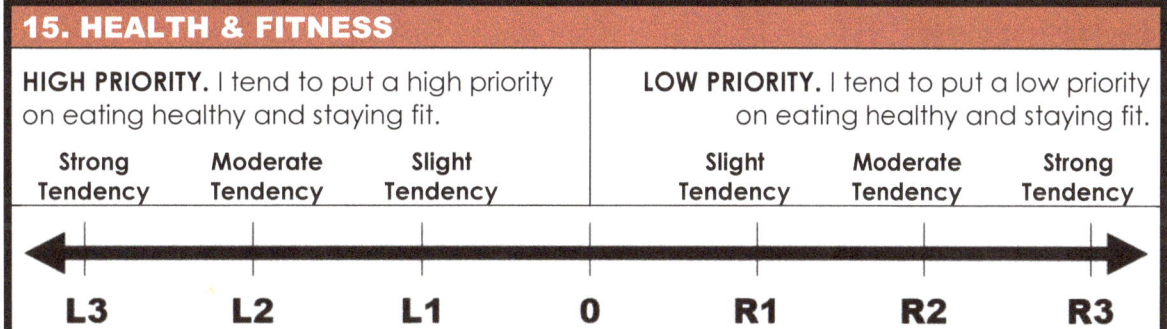

15. HEALTH & FITNESS

HIGH PRIORITY. I tend to put a high priority on eating healthy and staying fit.

LOW PRIORITY. I tend to put a low priority on eating healthy and staying fit.

Strong Tendency	Moderate Tendency	Slight Tendency		Slight Tendency	Moderate Tendency	Strong Tendency
L3	L2	L1	0	R1	R2	R3

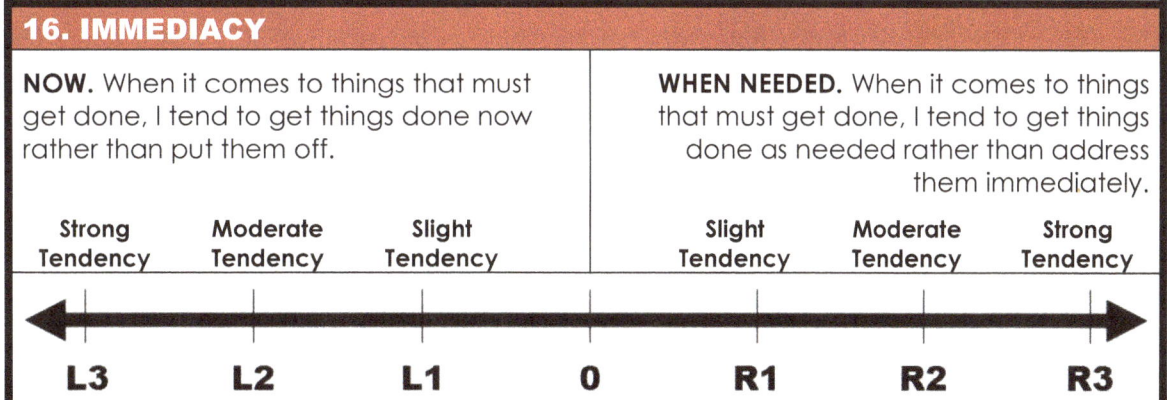

16. IMMEDIACY

NOW. When it comes to things that must get done, I tend to get things done now rather than put them off.

WHEN NEEDED. When it comes to things that must get done, I tend to get things done as needed rather than address them immediately.

Strong Tendency	Moderate Tendency	Slight Tendency		Slight Tendency	Moderate Tendency	Strong Tendency
L3	L2	L1	0	R1	R2	R3

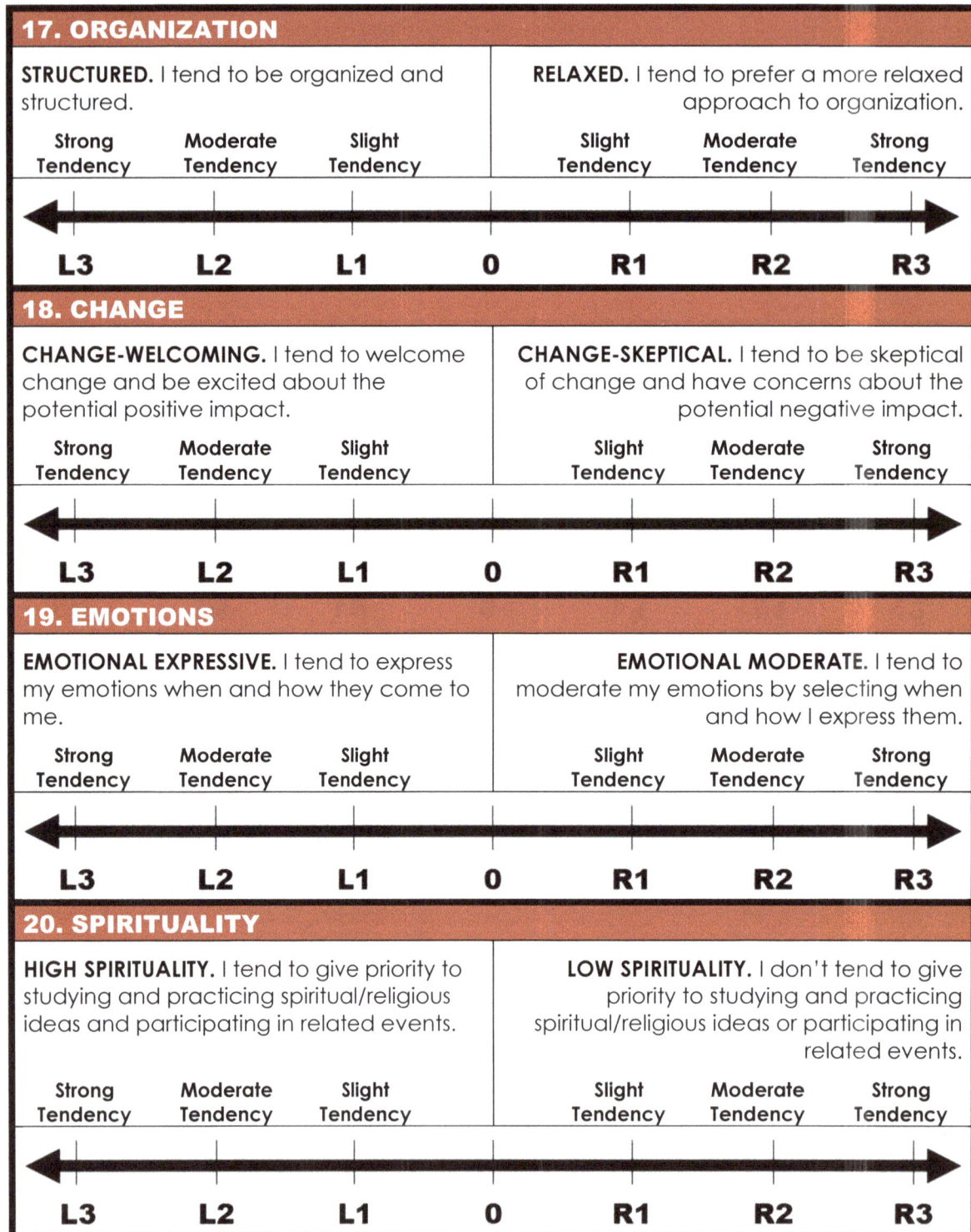

17. ORGANIZATION

STRUCTURED. I tend to be organized and structured.

RELAXED. I tend to prefer a more relaxed approach to organization.

Strong Tendency	Moderate Tendency	Slight Tendency		Slight Tendency	Moderate Tendency	Strong Tendency
L3	L2	L1	0	R1	R2	R3

18. CHANGE

CHANGE-WELCOMING. I tend to welcome change and be excited about the potential positive impact.

CHANGE-SKEPTICAL. I tend to be skeptical of change and have concerns about the potential negative impact.

Strong Tendency	Moderate Tendency	Slight Tendency		Slight Tendency	Moderate Tendency	Strong Tendency
L3	L2	L1	0	R1	R2	R3

19. EMOTIONS

EMOTIONAL EXPRESSIVE. I tend to express my emotions when and how they come to me.

EMOTIONAL MODERATE. I tend to moderate my emotions by selecting when and how I express them.

Strong Tendency	Moderate Tendency	Slight Tendency		Slight Tendency	Moderate Tendency	Strong Tendency
L3	L2	L1	0	R1	R2	R3

20. SPIRITUALITY

HIGH SPIRITUALITY. I tend to give priority to studying and practicing spiritual/religious ideas and participating in related events.

LOW SPIRITUALITY. I don't tend to give priority to studying and practicing spiritual/religious ideas or participating in related events.

Strong Tendency	Moderate Tendency	Slight Tendency		Slight Tendency	Moderate Tendency	Strong Tendency
L3	L2	L1	0	R1	R2	R3

Comparing Responses

For each of the twenty dimensions, review the degree of difference between your score and your partner's.

Difference	Example	Explanation
0	You both chose L2.	**No difference.** You are aligned on this dimension.
1-2	One of you chose L1 and the other chose L2 (difference of 1) or R1 (difference of 2), as shown in the sample comparison below.	**Slight difference.** You might not even notice this difference. When this difference does appear, intervention strategies will likely be sufficient.
3-4	One of you chose L2 and the other chose R1 (difference of 3) or R2 (difference of 4), as shown in the sample.	**Moderate difference.** These differences may show up from time to time and either proactive or intervention strategies may be sufficient to address them.
5-6	One of you chose L3 and the other chose R2 (difference of 5) or R3 (difference of 6).	**Significant difference.** You may frequently experience issues related to this difference and both proactive and intervention strategies should be considered.

Sample Comparison

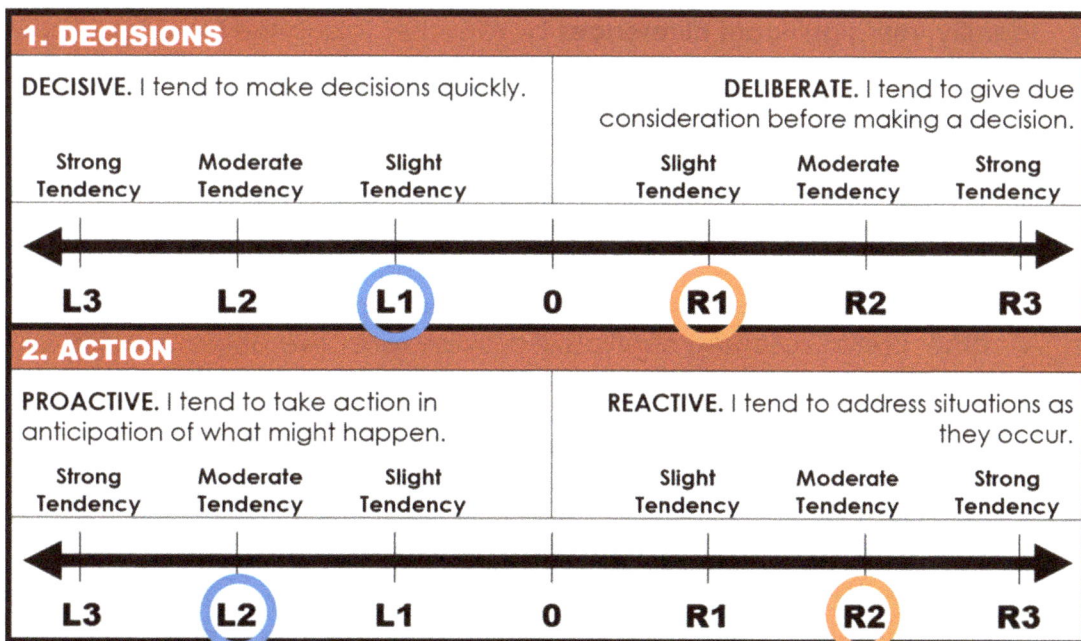

Managing differences starts very early for us. Even the families we are born into inevitably force us to confront differences with others. We often learn early in life the strategies that we will use later when faced with differences with others, especially those close to us.

Consider exploring the deeper questions that follow which may help you gain a better understanding of why you address differences in your relationship in the way that you do.

- What differences did you see between your parents, or primary caregivers? How did they manage them?
- In what ways were you different from your family members growing up?
- How were the differences handled?
- How were you treated because of the differences?
- How did that make you feel and what did you do about it?
- How did you manage differences in your past romantic partner relationships?
- How successful were you at managing differences and what do you wish you had done differently?

From these questions, and given your past experiences, do you notice any similarities or differences with how you feel and manage differences with your partner today?

Proactive Strategies

Let's focus now on proactive strategies for managing the differences.

1. **Identify your significant differences** by together taking the Couples Tendency Profile.
   - After taking the survey highlight any dimension where the difference is three points or more.
   - Consider looking back at your DISC styles to identify how the tendency difference may be reflective of a difference in your styles.
   - As an example, if you are three points or more different on the conflict dimension—that is, one person prefers avoiding conflicts, while the other prefers resolving conflicts, it may be reflective of the avoider being a high-S or high-C, while the resolver may be a high-D or high-I.

2. **Seek solutions that honor the key needs of both of you.** Use the consensus building strategies that you will learn in Principle 6, Addressing conflict.
   - As an example, if your partner tends to be conflict-tolerant and you tend to be conflict-resolving, your experience might be that you typically want to know about an issue early so the two of you can quickly resolve it, while you partner typically doesn't want to bring up issues because they perceive them as being not such a big deal or not worth the effort.

- In seeking solutions, you may agree that when a conflict is apparent to either of you, you will seek to bring it up and the other partner will seek to always thank the partner for sharing, and then together you will decide a time to talk about it for further understanding, without the pressure of having to get to a solution right away.

3. **Establish creative approaches that work for the two of you in communicating and resolving differences.**

   - Recognizing and communicating when a difference is showing up is a critical piece. Having a strategy to address a difference is also important, as you will see when I talk about intervention strategies.

Personal Insight	Michael and I learned early in our relationship that there was a small difference in our love languages.

Michael and I learned early in our relationship that there was a small difference in our love languages.

My top three:
1. Quality time
2. Words of affirmation
3. Touch

His top three
1. Touch
2. Words of affirmation
3. Quality time

As you can see, while we shared the second love language, words of affirmation, my number 1 was his number 3, and my 3 was his 1. This 1-3/3-1 difference showed up early in our relationship. When he was feeling emotionally distant from me he needed touch, and when I was feeling emotionally distant from him I needed quality time. These different needs would clash from time to time until we recognized how the difference was playing out and put in place proactive strategies to address it. What was our creative approach?

- First, we were able to name and talk about the difference when it showed up, "This is feeling like our 1-3/3-1 difference showing up."
- Once we identified it, we could talk about how we could address the difference so that both of us felt our love tank filling up.
- One of our favorite strategies is something we call "Scale It." The purpose of scaling is to communicate how strong your need is at the moment. Our scale is 1-to-10, with 10 being the strongest. When a difference manifested itself (e.g., I may be needing to spend time out together, but Michael may be needing to work late and looking forward to cuddling in bed), we would ask each other to scale the need. We both recognized that if a need for either of us was an 8 or higher, the other partner would make every effort to address that need.

4. **It's OK to grieve over the loss of tendencies that you wish your partner shared with you that you may have shared with previous partners**. But be open to seeing 1) how the differences can make your relationship different and unique, and 2) how the differences may be a strength for balancing you both and can help determine roles in the relationship.

Intervention Strategies

How do you recover if you or your partner has rejected rather than embraced a difference?

1. **Request a redo.**

   One of the fastest and easiest ways I teach couples to intervene during conflict is to say, "Stop. Can I have a redo and start over?" Emotional reactions are what typically happen automatically, so everyone is prone to a "slip" here and there. As soon as you or your partner are aware that you are not managing a difference well, activate this strategy!

2. **Practice assertive communication.**

   Slow things down by practicing the three main components of assertive communication:

   - Use I-statements.
     - For example, instead of saying, "You always need something from me," an appropriate I-statement might be, "I feel overwhelmed when you ask me to take care of your responsibilities."
     - I-statements reflect your thoughts and feelings to your partner. Using I-statements instead of You-statements helps disarm your partner and discourages them from reacting with defensive behaviors.
   - Use feeling words.
     - Your partner is more likely to respond to you in a more loving way when you share a vulnerable feeling with them instead of blaming them for something and expecting them to respond in an empathic way.
     - I find that people often have difficulty identifying their deeper, more vulnerable feelings to their partner. Therefore, I recommend partners have a "feelings wheel"[5] handy to help them identifying their deeper emotions. (You can download a feelings wheel by doing a search on this term using your favorite search engine.)

---

[5] Gloria Wilcox, "The Feeling Wheel: A Tool for Expanding Awareness of Emotions and Increasing Spontaneity and Intimacy," *Transactional Analysis Journal*, October 1, 1982, 274-276.

Feelings Wheel (small version)

(https://lifegifts.net/products/feeling-wheel-poster?)

- Ask specifically for what you need.
  - A vague request can leave your partner feeling lost and not knowing what action to take. Therefore it is important that your request be specific as opposed to vague and general. This will help your partner understand how they can help you most effectively in the here and now.
  - For example, instead of saying, "I need to feel loved by you," say, "Will you come close and wrap your arms around me, so I feel your love?"

3. **Use reflective listening.**
   - Couples frequently make faulty assumptions about what their partner's words and/or actions mean.
   - When you and your partner are navigating through a difference, it can be very helpful to restate your partner's message often to let them know you understand them clearly before you move through the discussion. This strategy can drastically reduce unnecessary misunderstandings.

     Examples of how to start a reflective listening statement
     - *What I hear you saying is ...*
     - *Let me make sure I have this right ...*
     - *It sounds like what you are saying is .... Is that right?*

- There may be times when your partner is not communicating with words. You can use reflective listening to reflect back the behavior you see versus what you hear. For example, you might say:
  - *I noticed you have been really quiet all day...*

4. **Seek solutions that respect the differences.**
   - In seeking solutions, you will want to use strategies we cover in Principle 6, Addressing conflict, for creating solutions to resolve conflict.
   - In seeking solutions, it is also important to avoid **A/B thinking**. A/B thinking occurs when one partner suggests A and the other suggests B, and the couple gets stuck arguing A versus B. Yet if they opened their discussion to seek other alternatives, they might find that there are other options (C, D, and E) that might be even better.

5. **Monitor the intervention for success.**
   - After you have implemented strategies to address a difference, be sure to check back in with each other to gain key learnings.
     - Was the strategy effective?
     - Is there more that needs to be done now to address this issue?
     - Is there a way we could have implemented the strategy to have made it even more effective?
     - Is there something we can do to help prevent the strategy from being needed in the future?

Summary and Close

Let's recap what we covered in this principle.

- In the introduction, I revisited Pam and Marcus and discussed a couple of differences in their lives.
- I then talked about communication styles and style differences, and a key tool we use, The Couples Tendency Profile, to identify important differences.
- From there, I revealed four proactive strategies to help you and your partner manage the differences and a five-step intervention strategy should one of you mismanage a difference.

Differences between individuals in a relationship are inevitable. The goal of this section has been to help you understand key differences you and your partner may have and provide you with strategies for addressing them. I want to close with four final points.

1. **Pay attention to your tone and body language.** In communication with others, your tone, that is, the way you say what you say, matters significantly. In fact, in many communications your tone is more important than the actual words you use. For example, the words, "That was interesting," could mean that it was completely fascinating, slightly entertaining, or completely boring, depending upon your tone. Likewise,

your body language can communicate volumes to people. When you and your partner are managing a difference, addressing a fire starter, resolving a disagreement, or repairing a rupture, pay careful attention to your tone and body language to ensure they are communicating the message you intend.

> **If you spend most of your time dwelling on how you and your partner are different, it can give undue attention to the challenging aspects of the relationship. Before you know it, when you think about your partner, your first thoughts will be about your negative feelings rather than the positive ones that brought you together.**

2. **Don't dwell on the dysfunction.** There is a spiritual catch phrase that says, "Where the attention goes, the power flows." It is likely that you and your partner are together for many positive reasons. However, as described before under the Power of Thinking, if you spend most of your time dwelling on how you are different, it can give undue attention to the challenging aspects of the relationship. Before you know it, when you think about your partner, your first thoughts will be your negative feelings rather than the positive ones that brought you together. My point isn't that it is bad to think about the differences. Just don't dwell on them. Recognize them and use the proactive and intervention strategies so that your focus stays on uplifting and bringing out the best in your partner.

3. **Differences can be magnified when away from the routine.** You may find that on vacations or during long weekends you and your partner appear to be especially prone to flare ups caused by a difference. This can happen because during those extended periods you don't have the everyday activities that allow you to avoid focusing on unresolved differences. These are especially good times to talk about difference and try new creative strategies to proactively address them (see the proactive strategies in this section).

4. **Always remember to honor your partner's difference.** Many times, it is the differences that help balance the relationship. The natural tendency is to think that your partner "should" be more like you. Far too often we look at differences in our partner as deficiencies in them, and we can think that they should be more like us. This kind of thinking can be very harmful because it can consciously or unconsciously communicate judgment or disapproval to your partner.

Instead, I believe you are better served by looking for ways that your partner's difference is valuable in the relationship.

- As an example, the conflict resolver might benefit from seeing that the conflict avoider's natural approach to life often allows the conflict avoider to accept small differences and keep the positive relationship flowing.

- On the other hand, the conflict avoider might benefit from seeing that the conflict resolver's natural approach prevents small issues from escalating into full scale ruptures in the relationship.

Differences between partners are real and should not be ignored. To create and sustain the lifelong honeymoon that you deserve, it is essential that you pay attention to differences and manage them well.

Practicing the Principle	With your partner, follow the directions to complete the Couples Tendency Profile documented in this principle.
	
	 For each of the dimensions where the difference is three or greater, ask:
	
	 • What is an example of where this difference has shown up in our relationship?
	
	 • In general, how well have we handled the difference? Consider rating on a 1-4 scale:
	
	    4-Very well
	
	    3-Adequately
	
	    2-Not so well
	
	    1-Poorly
	
	 • For any dimension where you rate the handling less than a 3, discuss what additional strategies you might use in the future to better manage this difference.

Notes

Notes

Principle 5:
Avoid the Fire Starters...They Can Ignite a Blaze

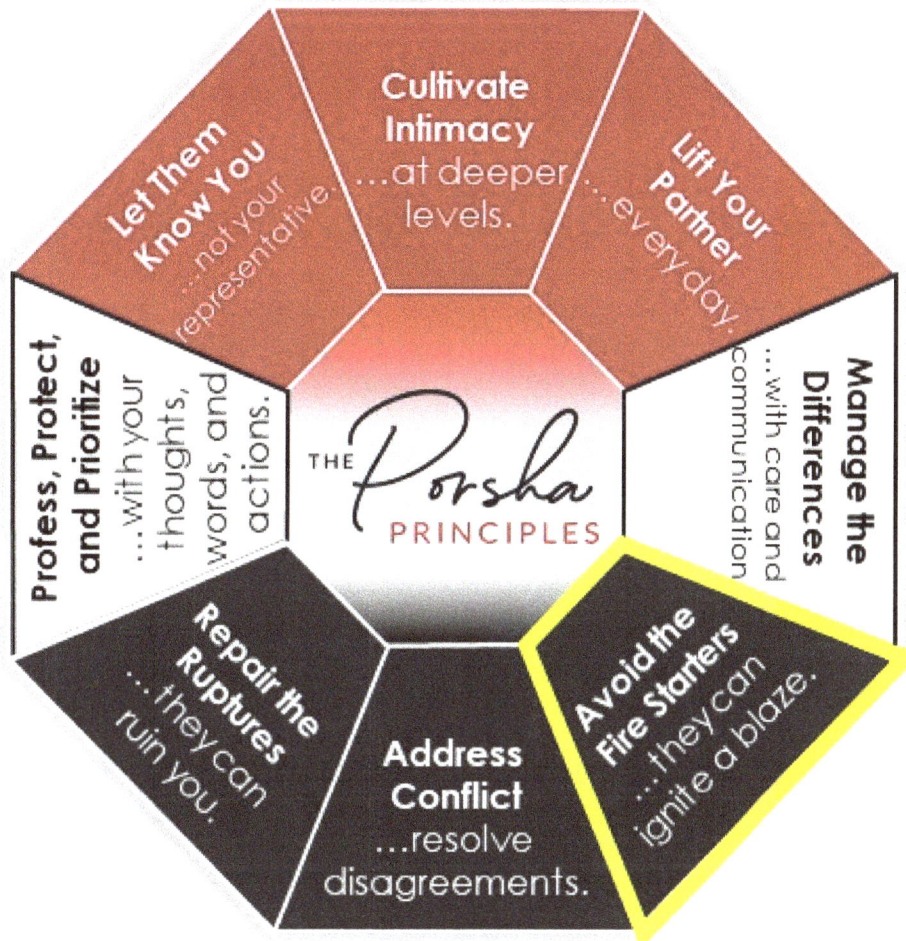

The Porsha Principles octagon diagram with the following sections:
- Cultivate Intimacy ...at deeper levels.
- Let Them Know You ...not your representative
- Lift Your Partner ...every day.
- Profess, Protect, and Prioritize ...with your thoughts, words, and actions.
- Manage the Differences ...with care and communication
- Repair the Ruptures ...they can ruin you.
- Address Conflict ...resolve disagreements.
- Avoid the Fire Starters ...they can ignite a blaze.

What You Will Learn	**Foundation**
	• What is a fire starter and what are the 14 most common ones?
	Proactive Strategies
	• What are the four fire prevention steps to prevent a fire before it starts?
	Intervention Strategies
	• What are the three steps to extinguish a fire you start before it turns into a blaze?
	• What are the four steps to extinguish a fire that your partner starts?
	Action
	• Steps you and your partner can take to put the principle into practice: "Our Fire Starters"

For every person, there are things their partner can do or say that nearly guarantee an argument will ensue. Do any of these statements resonate with you?

- *You're late, again?*
- *This wouldn't have happened if you had just listened to me!*
- *So, it's ALWAYS my fault?*
- *You are so narrow-minded sometimes.*
- *Why can't you just keep a commitment?*
- *You don't ever stand up for me.*
- *Blah, blah, blah.... I'm done talking about this.*
- *You always let your mother tell you what to do.*

I call statements like these fire starters. Why? They typically provoke your partner to respond in a negative way. You can likely recall a time when a statement like the ones above didn't stop with just the statement. Instead, it ignited a serious blaze that was difficult for the two of you to put out. Over time these negative experiences, if unresolved, can deteriorate into vicious cycles or severe ruptures, as you will learn in Principle 7, Repair the ruptures.

The Vicious Cycle

Let's take a closer look at how these cycles work.

When partners engage over and over in negative interactions, they create a negative behavior pattern that can become a vicious cycle. One partner does something that triggers a negative reaction from their partner, which then triggers another negative reaction from the other partner, which triggers … and so on. This vicious cycle can devastate the couple's attachment bond if the cycle is not disrupted.

Many times, couples are unaware of this vicious cycle; they are just trying to deal with all the day-to-day stuff and get their emotional needs met the best way they can. But any time one partner initiates a fire starter, or each time one partner tries to reach for the other and feels in some way rejected or unheard, the cycle is reactivated.

Often panic and fear are driving the vicious cycle. One or both partners is wondering, "Do I even matter to you? Do you have my back? Will you really be there for me?" There is a "cry for help," but usually it's an unhealthy cry, aka a fire starter such as blaming, criticizing or shaming, that continues to reactivate the cycle.

What pulls couples into the negative cycle? Let's look at what one of the legends in the therapy field has said about it.

The Four Horsemen of the Apocalypse

Dr. John Gottman, an American psychologist and world-renowned researcher known for his work on marital stability and his ability to predict the likelihood of divorce, isolated four fire starters which he called, "The Four Horsemen of the Apocalypse." If left unaddressed they can lead to the end of your relationship. Dr. Gottman has predicted relationship failure with over 90% accuracy when these behaviors aren't changed! Here is how he describes these harmful behaviors.

Criticism	• An attack on your partner at the core of their character *(not just their behavior)* *Your never think of anyone but yourself. You are so selfish.*
Contempt	• Treating your partner with disrespect, sarcasm, ridicule, or mocking behaviors; contempt assumes a position of superiority *You call yourself a man? A real man provides for his family. You are just a little boy in a man's body.*
Defensiveness	• A response to a perceived attack that attempts to invalidate or diminish your partner's thoughts, feelings, or actions. *Of course I forgot to pick that up on my way home. I have so much on my mind from work, how can I possibly remember something like that?*
Stone Walling	• Withdrawing from the interaction, shutting down, or not responding to your partner. *I'm done! I don't want to waste another second on this.*

Additional Fire Starters

Along with the four fire starters from Dr. Gottman, in discussing this principle I want to describe nine other common fire starters I've seen through my many years of treating couples. I counter these additional fire starters with strategies for preventing the fire from starting in the first place, and then intervention strategies for quickly extinguishing them.

Blaming	Blaming occurs when a person makes their partner feel guilty for a mistake the partner made. Oftentimes blame is done to cover up one's own mistake (deflecting). *That was a huge mistake you made.*
Deflecting	Deflection occurs when a partner tries to shift attention away from themselves to their partner or someone else in order to avoid taking responsibility for their action. *Yeah, I made a mistake, but it's because of you that we are in this situation in the first place.*
Exaggerating	Exaggerating occurs when a partner uses a superlative or a gross overstatement to make a point against their partner. *You never talk to me, you never listen to me, you never give me the time of day.*
Gaslighting	Gaslighting occurs when a partner attempts to avoid responsibility for their action by making the other partner question their own judgement or view of reality. *No, I never said that. You made that up. You always make things up.*
Guilting	Guilting occurs when one partner tries to induce the feeling of guilt in the other partner in order to get their way. *You spend so much time at work. But when I want just a little of your time, you don't have it for me.*
Keeping Score	Keeping score is a me-centered way of operating, by which you're elevating your role in the relationship to a place of superiority through showing (or claiming) that you have done more than the other person. *Every time you travel for work, I have to do my job and take care of the kids solo, so when it comes to vacation, we should do what I want to do.*
Shaming	Shaming combines blaming and guilting. It's an attack on your partner's behavior that isn't in accord with your expectations and adds an underlying message of guilt related to the behavior. *That was a huge mistake you made. You should be ashamed of yourself.*
Shoulding	Shoulding occurs when the partner uses should or shouldn't to express a set of rules of how things should have been done or should be done in the future. Shoulding often comes with an underlying sense of judgment or superiority. *See what happens when you let things go to the last minute? You shouldn't do that.*
Speaking out of anger	Speaking out of anger toward your partner includes threats, yelling, shouting, name calling, and the use of profanity. *Just shut the hell up!*

> ### Deeper Dive
>
> Our method of engaging with other people when we are upset often comes from the modeling we saw as children. For example, if you come from a family that was very emotionally expressive and reactive, you may find your tendency is to do the same—react first, think second. Consider exploring these deeper questions which may help you better understand why your tendencies are what they are when it comes to fire starters.
>
> - Think about you as a child growing up. How did your parents or primary caregivers communicate with each other when they were upset?
> - How did each of them communicate with you when they were upset with you? (e.g., being critical, blaming, shaming)
> - Whether they were communicating with you or each other, how did that make you feel?
> - What did you do about it?
> - How did you communicate to partners in past intimate relationships when you were upset? How do you feel about that? What do you wish you had done differently?
>
> From these questions, and given your past experiences, do you notice any similarities or differences with how you communicate when upset with your partner today?

Proactive Strategies

Use proactive strategies to prevent the fire before it starts. If you find **yourself** about to deliver a fire starter, try my **4-step Fire Prevention Strategy**.

1. Pause ... count to five before you respond to allow time for the automatic negative reaction to pass.

2. Next, quickly remind yourself how much your partner means to you and how much you care about them.

3. Then consider the reaction you most desire from your partner (e.g., an apology, an expression of concern for you, a change in their behavior, etc.)

4. Finally, decide the words to use that would most likely evoke that reaction from your partner.

You may be surprised how these four simple steps can help extinguish a fire even before it starts. These steps can truly be an effective fire prevention strategy.

If you are unable to stay calm enough to use the fire prevention strategy, protect your relationship by calling a timeout and coming back to the table at an agreed upon time. Here's an example:

I want to take a timeout here. I'm starting to get irritated, and I know I won't be able to engage in a healthy conversation right now. This is important, so can we come back to this in a few hours once I have had chance to think about it more and calm down?

During that timeout period, keep reminding yourself that your partner is not you. They are different, not necessarily wrong. When you come back together focus on these four things:

- Practice gratitude.
- Talk openly about your needs and expectations.
- Practice active listening by listening to understand and provide feedback, instead of listening to react.
- Address your concerns in an assertive way with your partner.

Remember, you can't control how your partner reacts to you, but you can control how you react to your partner.

Intervention Strategies

Use intervention strategies to extinguish the fire before it becomes a blaze. **If you find that you have delivered a fire starter to your partner**, immediately begin this 3-step extinguishing strategy.

Fire Extinguishing Strategy #1 (If you have delivered a fire starter):

1. Request a redo. *Stop. Can I have a redo and start over?*

2. Slow things down and apologize.

   I am frustrated and overreacted just now. I am sorry.

3. Practice assertive communication.
   - Use I-statements.
   - Use feeling words.
   - Ask specifically for what you need.

   It would be helpful to me if you would lower your voice and let me know that you are hearing me. What did you hear me say?

If your partner delivers a fire starter to you, rather than ignite the blaze, consider this 4-step extinguishing strategy.

Fire Extinguishing Strategy #2 (if your partner has delivered a fire starter)

1. Let your partner know the primary emotion you are feeling. (It's a good time to refer to your feeling wheel.) Let's take an example of your partner using the blaming fire starter.

   When you say it that way, I feel very blamed, and it makes it hard for me to hear you.

2. Ask your partner if they can state what they need using I-statements instead of a fire starter.

It's pretty apparent that you are upset, and I am sorry for that. We've talked before about I-statements and that seems to work for us. I would appreciate it if you could use an I-statement to tell me how you are feeling or what you need from me.

3. Continue using the assertive communication and reflective listening strategies described in Principle 4, Managing the differences, to extinguish the fire starter.

    *   Use I-statements.
    *   Use feeling words.
    *   Ask specifically for what you need.

4. Restate your partner's message often to let them know you understand them clearly before you move through the discussion.

    *   What I hear you saying is ...
    *   Let me make sure I have this right ...
    *   It sounds like what you are saying is.... Is that right?

Once more, if you are unable to stay calm enough to use the fire extinguishing strategy, protect your relationship by calling a timeout and coming back to the table at an agreed upon time.

My clients often tell me that the first step is the hardest: remembering in the heat of the moment to find their words for healthy communication to evoke the desired response they want from their partner. So below for each of the fire starters I have provided sample words you might use to take the first step to extinguish the fire.

Extinguishing Responses: The First Step

	Fire Starter	Extinguishing Response
Blaming	*That was a huge mistake you made.*	*When you say it that way I feel very blamed, and it makes it hard for me to hear you.*
Criticism	*Your never think of anyone but yourself. You are so selfish.*	*When you call me selfish, I feel criticized and hurt, and it makes me want to end the conversation.*
Contempt	*You call yourself a man? A real man provides for his family. You are just a little boy in a man's body.*	*That statement makes me feel so hurt and disrespected. I need to call a timeout.*
Defensiveness	*Of course I forgot to pick that up on my way home. I have so much on my mind from work, how could I possibly remember something like that?*	*I feel hurt because I counted on you and it feels like you are saying that it's my fault, instead of apologizing for forgetting.*

	Fire Starter	Extinguishing Response
Deflecting	Yeah I made a mistake, but it's because of you that we are in this situation in the first place.	When I am talking about a concern I have and you bring up a concern you have, it makes me feel like my concern doesn't matter to you and it makes it hard for me to hear you.
Exaggerating	You never talk to me, you never listen to me, you never give me the time of day.	When you say "never" it makes feel disheartened and hopeless, and that none of my actions in the past have pleased you.
Gaslighting	No, I never said that. You made that up. You always make things up.	When you deny what I know to be a fact, I feel lied to and manipulated by you.
Guilting	You spend so much time at work. But when I want just a little of your time, you don't have it for me.	When you say that it makes me upset because it seems that you are trying to guilt me into doing what you want me to do.
Keeping score	Every time you travel for work, I have to do my job and take care of the kids solo, so when it comes to vacation, we should do what I want to do.	When you say that I feel frustrated because it sounds like you have been keeping score and I can never catch up.
Shaming	That was a huge mistake you made. You should be ashamed of yourself.	When you say that I feel really hurt that someone I love would want me to feel ashamed for making a mistake.
Shoulding	See what happens when you let things go to the last minute? You shouldn't do that.	When you "should" me like that I feel very judged by you, and it makes it hard for me to hear you.
Speaking out of anger	Just shut the hell up!	When you speak to me that way, I feel very disrespected. I need to take a timeout.
Stonewalling	I'm done! I don't want to waste another second on this.	When you say that I feel dismissed and belittled and that my needs aren't important to you.

What if My Partner Is Not Willing to Change?

I often get the question, "What can I do if my partner is not willing to change?" Of course, it is important to first ask yourself, "Am **I** willing to change?" If you want someone to change their behavior, you must first be willing to change yours. To have a chance at a lifelong honeymoon requires two partners who are willing to do the work of understanding each other's needs, identifying behaviors that get in the way, and adjusting as needed to continue to positively contribute to the love pool.

Unfortunately, if your partner is unwilling to change, your options become fairly limited. Here are three to consider.

1. Do the things that have the potential to increase their willingness (e.g., couples counseling, speaking with your pastor, or seeking input from other, healthy couples that your partner trusts).
2. Accept or tolerate the behavior.
3. Leave the relationship.

If your partner is not willing to participate in even the first step, it may be helpful for you to seek individual counseling to get assistance for yourself around steps two or three. While this is not a service we provide at Porsha Principles, on our website you will find trusted referral partners who may be able to help.

Summary and Close

Let's recap what we covered in this principle.

- I started with talking about what is a fire starter and examining 13 of the most common ones.
- I described the four-step fire prevention strategy and the three steps to extinguish a fire you started before it turns into a blaze.
- I also talked about the four steps to extinguish a fire your partner starts.

As described in this principle, if your goal is to have a lifelong honeymoon it is essential that you and your partner:

- Eliminate fire starters as much as possible in your relationship.
- Extinguish fire starters that do occur as quickly as possible to avoid igniting a blaze.

Finally, keep in mind these things.

- Start with the thought that your partner has the best intentions.
- Recognize that everyone makes mistakes, and we all don't always show up at our best.
- Be willing to give your partner the benefit of the doubt and be willing to forgive and let go and move past the event once it has been addressed.
- Don't dwell on the dysfunction; if you find yourself thinking about a fire starter that has already been addressed, move past it by shifting your

mind to positive attributes about your partner. (You will hear more about shifting your thoughts under Principle 8, Profess, protect, and renew the relationship ... with your thoughts, words, and actions.)

- Be teachable; be open to taking in new information as objectively as possible; be willing to look at something from a different angle as opposed to assuming that your partner is wrong or intending to hurt you when they give you feedback.

Eliminating and productively addressing fire starters is another key step in building your lifelong honeymoon.

Practicing the Principle	**Fire Drill: Practice in Extinguishing Fires**
	You and your partner can practice extinguishing fires. By practicing outside the heat of the moment, you can build "muscle memory" that you can use when it really counts.

1. Start by having each partner identify one or more fire starters that the other partner sometimes employs.

2. After identifying one or more fire starters, write down three examples of statements similar to something the partner might say that could ignite a fire. The statements can be different forms of the same fire starter, or they can be for different fire starters. The words don't have to be exactly what your partner has said in the past, just something similar.

3. Note: Avoid getting defensive during this stage if you don't believe the fire starter statement is something you have said or would say. The point is for your partner to have an opportunity to practice responding to different fire starters should they occur.

4. The Role Play:
   - **Fire Starter**: Each partner takes turns saying one of the fire starters your partner picked for you.
   - **Fire Extinguisher**: The other partner then practices responding with Fire Extinguisher #2 outlined above.
   - **Fire Starter**: The fire starter then responds in a positive way to the fire extinguisher's words, such as:
     - *Okay, sorry about that.*
     - *Oh, let me say that in a different way.*
     - *Thank you, I didn't mean that at all. What I really want from you is ...*
     - *Can you help me say it in a way so that you can hear me?*
   - **Exchange roles** and do it again.

After going through three rounds of each partner being the fire starter, discuss together what it felt like being in each role and how you can use the role play experience when addressing actual fire starting/fire extinguishing experiences in your relationship.

Notes

Principle 6:
Address Conflicts ... Resolve Disagreements.

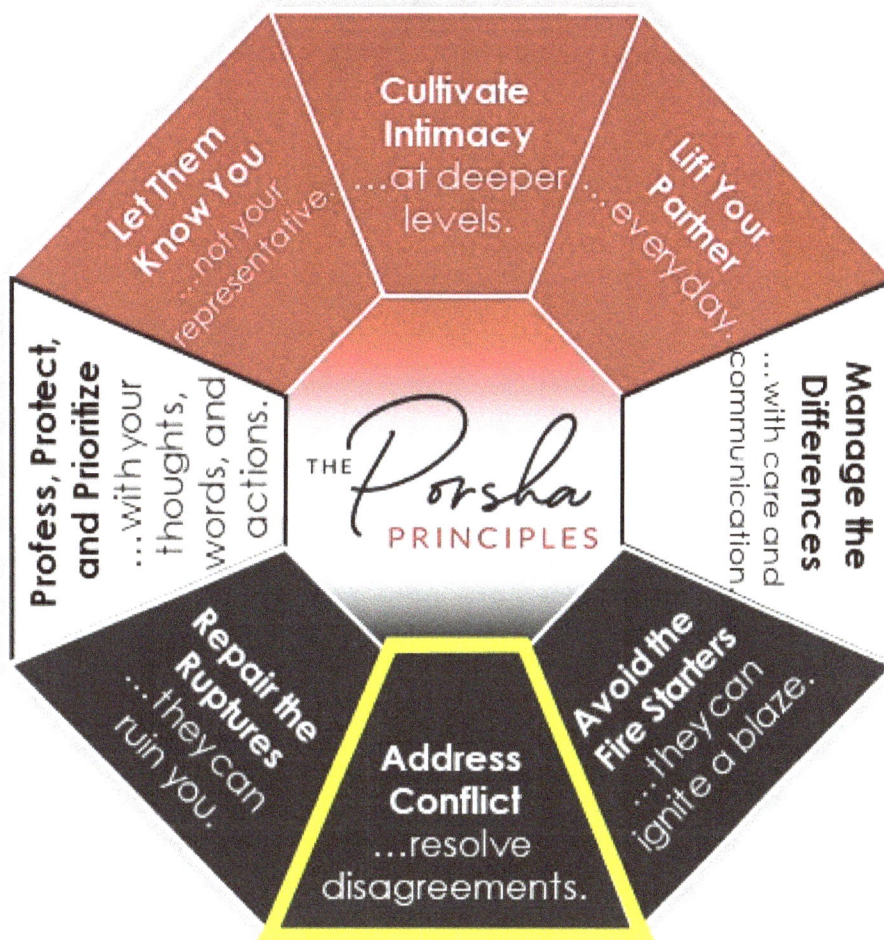

What You Will Learn	**Foundation** • The three reasons people disagree and the causes of each **Intervention Strategies** • Three steps for resolving a level-1 disagreement • Eight steps for resolving a level-2 disagreement • How to recognize level-3 disagreements and the five steps to addressing them **Action Strategies** • Steps you and your partner can take to put the principle into practice: Categorizing Our Past Disagreements

Introduction

Conflict occurs when differences or disagreements are not handled well. In Principle 4 we talked about strategies for avoiding conflict by managing the differences. In this principle we will focus on strategies for addressing disagreements, because unresolved disagreements can lead to major conflicts in your relationship.

Disagreements happen in relationships. Any time two people are together who have different goals, values, and life experiences, they will invariably have different perspectives and beliefs about what should be done to address the various situations that occur in life.

Disagreements are indeed inevitable. But one of the things that separates couples on their way to a lifelong honeymoon from those who are not is how effectively they deal with disagreements. Some couples are lucky and intuitively discover effective strategies for addressing their disagreements. This principle is for the rest of us:

- Those who find their relationship in a constant ditch because of unresolved disagreements.
- Those who avoid discussing certain topics because they know it will result in a blow up.
- Those who are just tired of battling all the time.

> **Here is some good news: There are only three reasons people disagree!**

Disagreement Types

Here's some good news. Did you know that there are only three reasons people disagree? Every disagreement in a relationship can be classified as a level-1, level-2, or level-3 disagreement.

- Level 1: Lack of shared information
- Level 2: Different values
- Level 3: Personality, past history, or other outside factors

Couples can benefit by understanding these types of disagreements and by having strategies for resolving them.

But there is also some bad news. If you are having a level-3 disagreement and you try to address it using level-1 techniques, you will likely fail. Level-3 disagreements can't be solved with level-1 techniques. Likewise, if you and your partner are having a level-1 disagreement and you try to resolve it by using level-2 techniques, your chances of success are also very, very low.

In this principle we will examine the three reasons people disagree and identify specific techniques that you can begin using immediately to resolve each type of disagreement.

> *Note:* *This principle is adapted from Michael's book,* The Secrets of Facilitation.[6] *You can check out his book for more insights on managing disagreements.*

Level-1 Disagreements: Lack of Shared Information

In my experience, I have found that most disagreements with couples are indeed level-1 disagreements: there is a lack of shared information. Fortunately, level-1 disagreements are also the easiest to resolve.

What is the cause? With level-1 disagreements, the people disagreeing have not clearly heard or understood each other's alternative and the reasons for supporting it. Level-1 disagreements are often a result of assumed understanding of what the other person is saying or meaning. Take a look at this level-1 disagreement between Pam and Marcus.

Sample Disagreement: Getting Together with Friends

Marcus:	Last night with Janice and Derrick was a disaster. I don't think we should ever go out with them again.
Pam:	No, I can't agree with that.
Marcus:	Look, her husband's a jerk. You even said so yourself on our drive home. It's just not fun being with them.
Pam:	No, I am not ready to write them off. You are just being anti-social.
Marcus:	Anti-social? Come on, Pam, that's unfair. I just don't like the guy and I don't understand why you would ever want to go out with them again.
Pam:	Look, with just about every couple we know, we like one of them more than the other. What are we going to do? Not have any friends who are couples? Plus, Janice is my best friend from college, and I am not going to stop seeing her because her husband is more than a bit prickly. On top of that, I am her daughter's godmother. Am I supposed to not have involvement in her life? And ...
Marcus:	Hold on a second. I'm not sure you are hearing me. I said we shouldn't go out with them again, not stop seeing them. Janice is wonderful and a great friend to you. Of course you should continue to see her and your goddaughter as often as you can. And it's fine to include both Janice

---

[6] Michael Wilkinson, The Secrets of Facilitation, 2nd Edition (San Francisco: Jossey-Bass, 2012, 209-246)

and Derrick when we have gatherings over our place or even when we have group dates with other couples because …

Pam: Right, even when we have group dates with other couples, because we wouldn't be stuck with having to interact with him all night. I get it. That makes sense, so why didn't you say that in the first place?

Marcus: I did say it, you just weren't listening. I said, I don't think we should ever go out with them again. What did you think I meant?

It is clear what Pam thought Marcus meant. Pam assumed that the words "I don't think we should ever go out with them" meant that Marcus didn't want either of them to ever see the couple again. She didn't realize that Marcus really was talking only about having one-on-one dates with her best friend and her husband. Once she understood what Marcus meant, she quickly agreed.

Did you notice when the tone of the conversation changed? There was a statement made that shifted the entire conversation. You might think it occurred when Marcus said, "Hold on a second. I'm not sure you are hearing me." But the transition actually happened before then.

> **When two people argue, each of them is making statements to support their argument. They are talking at each other rather than to each other. If either party were to step back and begin asking questions, the talking at each other would stop and listening would begin.**

See, typically when two people argue, each of them is in advocacy mode. They are each making statements to support their argument. They are talking **at** each other rather than **to** each other. If either party were to step back and go into inquiry mode and begin asking questions, the talking at each other would stop and listening would begin.

When did the change in the conversation occur? When Marcus said, "I don't understand why you would ever want to go out with them again." Notice that even though it is a statement, it really is an implied question: "Why would you ever want to go out with them again?" Once Marcus actually asks the implied question, Pam responds, and this leads to the recognition that they were not in disagreement at all. They simply didn't understand one another at first.

The authors of *Crucial Conversations*[7] used the term "violent agreement" to describe this kind of disagreement. The parties really agree, but they don't know it, so they continue arguing. One of the common statements heard at the resolution of a level-1 disagreement is, "Oh, is that what you meant? Why didn't you say that?"

---

[7] Joseph Grenny, Kerry Patterson, Al Switzler, Ron McMillan, *Crucial Conversations: Tools for Talking When Stakes Are High* (New York: McGraw Hill, 2002)

Solving Level-1 Disagreements

To solve a level-1 disagreement, couples must learn to move out of advocacy mode and use questions to slow down the conversation and encourage careful listening and understanding. When the disagreement is due solely to a lack of shared information, the parties quickly learn that they were not in disagreement at all. They were not hearing each other, hearing but not understanding, or not sharing relevant information.

> **If you find yourself disagreeing with something your partner says, slow down the conversation by building a PAC.**

If you find yourself disagreeing with something your partner says, and your sense is that it could be a source of conflict, slow down the conversation by doing what I call building a PAC.

Building a PAC

- **P**lay back what you believe you heard and confirm that you heard it correctly: *It sounds like you are saying … is that right?*
- **A**gree with what you can agree with: *I certainly agree that …*
- **C**hallenge by asking a question to address your concerns: *If we do this, how … or How would that work?*

Let's listen to that same conversation but this time with Pam building a PAC with Marcus.

Sample Disagreement: Getting Together with Friends (Building a PAC)

Marcus:	Last night with Janice and Derrick was a disaster. I don't think we should ever go out with them again.
Pam:	It sounds like you're saying you aren't interested in us continuing to spend time with them. Is that right?
Marcus:	Yes, her husband acts like a jerk sometimes. You even said so yourself on our drive home. It's just not fun being with them.
Pam:	I certainly can agree that Derrick can be a bit prickly, and so I can see why you wouldn't want to spend time with them. My concern is that I want to keep my relationship with Janice and my godchild. If we stop seeing them, how do I keep those relationships intact?
Marcus:	Of course you should continue to see Janice and your goddaughter as often as you can. And it's even fine to include both Janice and Derrick when we have gatherings over our place or when we have group dates with other couples. I just want to avoid us going out with them one-on-one. Will that work for you?
Pam:	That's probably a really good idea. I'm glad you thought of it. Hey, it's still early. Let's see if we can catch that movie you've been wanting to see.

Let's take a closer look at the three parts to building a PAC.

- **Playback**. You may think that the playback seems unnecessary. And in some cases that may be so. However, it might surprise you how often it is that when one person does a playback, the other says something akin to, "No, that's not what I am saying at all." And with that the Level 1 disagreement is resolved! But along with ensuring your understanding, when you use playback it also lets the other person know you are indeed hearing them. Sadly, in arguments far too many couples aren't listening to each other at all, but instead are waiting for the other person to stop so they can make their next point. Playback forces you and your partner to listen.

- **Agree**. Likewise, you may feel that it is disingenuous to agree with what you can agree with, even though you don't agree with all of what your partner said. Yet, by identifying positives in your partner's point, you are affirming once more that you have heard them and found some value in their point.

- **Challenge**. The challenge question tends to be the most difficult part for couples to implement. Remember my point earlier, when people argue they tend to be in advocacy mode instead of inquire mode. The challenge question is intended to have you ask a question that gives your partner the opportunity to address your concern.

  - As in the scenario, Pam was concerned about the impact on her relationship with her friend and goddaughter and so she asked the classic challenge question: **If we do this, how...**

  - In some cases, you might need to gather more information to confirm what you think might be a concern. In this case, ask the more general question, **How would that work?** and then listen closely as your partner describes what they have in mind. Once you are clear that you have a concern, ask your challenge question.

Level-2 Disagreements: Different Values

Level-2 disagreements are based on you and your partner having different values. These disagreements are significantly more difficult to address because the disagreement is based on a set of beliefs or experiences that is not shared by the other partner. Recall that a level-1 disagreement is resolved as soon as both parties identify the unshared information. This is not the case with level-2 disagreements. With these disagreements the parties have fully heard and understood one another's alternatives, but they hold different values that result in one person preferring one alternative and the other person preferring a different one.

Let's take a look at Pam and Marcus having a level-2 disagreement.

Sample Disagreement: Planning a Vacation

Pam	I've been thinking about our vacation for next year, and I've got it! There's a 10-day/7-city tour of Spain that includes Madrid, Valencia, Seville, and Barcelona. It's perfect. What do you think?
Marcus	That does sound like a wonderful tour. But I have really been looking forward to going to the beach this year.
Pam	Oh, come on, be my hero. Let's go to Spain. We haven't been there before. It'll be fun.
Marcus	Oh, sweetheart, darling, baby. Let's go to the beach. It'll be quiet and restful. I'll rub your back with suntan lotion.
Pam	Now, Marcus, you've been out of town a lot this year, which has left me home to do both my job and take care of the kids solo. So, we really should do what I want to do. Let's do Spain.
Marcus	You are right, Pam. I have been out of town a lot this year, and it has worn me out. I really need a break. Let's go to the beach.
Pam	No, we are going to Spain.
Marcus	No, we are going to the beach.
Pam	Spain!
Marcus	Beach!
Pam	Spain!

Clearly, Pam loves to travel. She values vacations that allow her to see many things and have many new and different experiences. For her, the ten-day, seven-city tour is ideal. Marcus, however, lives out of a suitcase for major parts of the year because he travels for his job. The last thing he wants to do when he is on vacation is to pack every morning to go to another hotel. (That sounds like what he does when he is working!) He wants the quiet, sandy beach. He wants to be able to sleep late most mornings, get up when he wants to get up, and do nothing if he wants to do nothing.

Let's examine this disagreement a little more closely.

- **Positions.** Pam and Marcus have both taken positions. Pam wants to go on a 10-day/7-city tour of Spain while Marcus wants to spend a week at the beach.
- **Likely outcome.** If the argument stays at the position level, the most likely outcome is win-lose: one of one of them is going to win and one of them is going to lose. In some cases, they can end up with lose-lose, where from frustration and anger Pam goes on her tour and Marcus goes to the beach: they both lose the benefit of the other's company.
- **Tip of the iceberg.** Think of positions as just the tip of the iceberg: what is really important is under the surface. These are the real issues or values that lie under the surface and explain why they feel as they do.

- **Getting under the surface.** The key to solving a level-2 disagreement is to isolate the key underlying values and create alternatives that combine the values. How do you do it? You may have guessed already: you ask questions and then you listen.

As an aside, while it appears that Pam and Marcus are arguing about where to go on vacation this year, if you lift up the cover on this argument, you will see that the disagreement is really about the purpose of vacation. For Pam, the purpose of vacation is excitement—going to new places, experiencing new things. For Marcus, the purpose of vacation is regeneration—having a chance to relax and recharge. Until they come to agreement on the purpose of vacation, they will have this disagreement <u>every single year</u>.

Solving Level-2 Disagreements

As mentioned earlier, to solve a level-2 disagreement isolate the key values and create an alternative that combines the values. Let's walk through the steps, assuming that they have already determined this is not a level-1 disagreement.

1. **Agree to try to resolve the disagreement using *The Porsha Principles* approach.** As an example, Pam might say: *This is an important issue. Might we try to apply* the Porsha Principles *with this?*

2. **Identify what you agree on and confirm the source of the disagreement.** Pam might continue by saying something like this, *We seem to agree that we want to be together on vacation. Where we seem to be disagreeing is on where we should go, right?*

3. **Confirm the alternatives and ask for others.** Continuing, Pam might say, *I'm wanting to take the 10-day/7-city tour of Spain and you're wanting to do a week at the beach, do I have that right? Are there other alternatives we should consider?* Other alternatives might not be so obvious yet, so it is not a problem if only the two alternatives are considered.

4. **Identify the strengths of each alternative**. Together, define the strengths of each alternative over the other one.

   I recommend that you actually create a T-bar on paper and write down the strengths of each alternative so that you both can see them. With Pam and Marcus, the T-bar might look like this.

Strengths	
10-Day / 7-City Tour of Spain	**7 Days on the Beach**
• Varied locations and cultures	• Relaxing
• Things we haven't seen before	• Sleeping in the same bed
• Variety of local activities	• No obligations
• Meeting new people	• Water sports

While at first you may find it helpful to have the <u>supporter</u> of the alternative identify its strength, after using this process a few times, you may find benefit in having the strengths of an alternative first identified by the person opposing it, and then having the other person point out any other strengths their partner did not. Having someone identify strengths of an option they oppose tends to open their minds to understanding and considering the needs of their partner.

5. **Identify the weaknesses of each alternative**. After identifying the strengths of each alternative, together identify the weaknesses of each one. Note that if there are only two alternatives, this step may not be necessary, as the strengths of one alternative will likely be the weaknesses of the other.

6. **Check for agreement.** Sometimes, identifying strengths and weaknesses is enough to convince one partner or the other that the other alternative is significantly better.

7. **Isolate the key strengths.** Have each partner identify the one or two most important strengths of their alternative. When Pam and Marcus did this step they identified the following as their key strengths.

(**KEY) Strengths	
10-Day / 7-City Tour of Spain	**7 Days on the Beach**
• **Varied locations and cultures****	• **Relaxing****
• **Things we haven't seen before****	• **Sleeping in the same bed****
• Variety of local activities	• No obligations
• Meeting new people	• Water sports

8. **Seek a merged alternative.** Ask: *Can we think of an alternative that combines these key strengths?* For Marcus and Pam, they quickly discovered that an alternative that allowed both of them to get their key strengths met: A cruise!

This example is taken from a couple that I happen to know. And since discovering their answer, they have gone on seven cruises! She gets the different ports of call; he gets to sleep in the same bed every night and relax most days. See, the strengths and merge technique can be quite effective!

I want to bring up two other important points.

- Recall that a level-2 disagreement is based on different values. When you ask people for the strengths of their alternative, their responses typically represent the values they hold, which in turn result in their preferring one alternative over the other. By identifying the strengths, you are actually identifying values. Thus, when you then follow up with the merge technique, you are actually creating a new alternative that combines your values. This can be a very powerful and helpful process to a couple who seem to be stuck between two competing alternatives.

- You might think of the merge technique as compromise, where people are giving up something to get something else. However, I believe it is not compromise at all; it is creativity. The process opens the mind to creating new alternatives that consider both your needs and the most important needs of your partner. You may be surprised at how it allows you to come up with creative ways to address seemingly difficult conflicts.

Personal Insight	**The Coin Flip** • There have been many times in our relationship where we recognized we were having a level-2 disagreement in which we fully understood each other's alternatives, preferred our own, but were open to the other. • Often in those cases, we say a prayer and ask our Creator to decide for us, and then we flip a coin. I suspect that might sound a bit unusual, but we have found it quite effective, especially when we are open to either alternative. • I vividly remember the first time it happened. We had gone on several dates, and we were growing very close. It was our first weekend together (I lived 30 miles away), and Michael had gotten me a hotel room so my "Pam the Protector" would feel safe … at least so he said! We had mutually agreed that neither of us were ready for our relationship to become intimate. • At his place that first evening, we had a great time talking and laughing together. Neither of us wanted the night to end. As we were readying to leave his place so he could drop me at the hotel, he invited me to stay as long as **I could** live up to our agreement (funny man). Though I fully trusted him and really wanted to stay, I told him I thought it would be best if I didn't. • He suggested the idea of leaving it to Spirit to decide if it was better for us to part for the evening or not. He suggested flipping a coin. I am a strong believer in the presence of Spirit, and I confidently said yes, thinking *I will call heads because Spirit would want me to make a head decision.* • It was tails, and we have been together ever since.

Level-3 Disagreements: Outside Factors

While level-1 disagreements are based on information and level-2 disagreements are based on values, level-3 disagreements are based on personality, past history, or other factors that have nothing to do with the disagreement. Let's listen to this level-3 disagreement.

Sample Disagreement: Celebrating a Promotion

Pam	Marcus, I'm home and I have some great news. I got the promotion!
Marcus	Baby, that's great! It's time to celebrate.
Pam	Agreed. Let's go to that new Italian restaurant, Fellini's.
Marcus	No, let's not go there.
Pam	What's wrong with Fellini's?

Marcus	Nothing, I just don't want to go.
Pam	I don't understand. Why don't you want to go?
Marcus	Look, I just don't want to, okay? Think of somewhere else.
Pam	You are so stubborn sometimes. It's my celebration, so why can't you just go along with what I want to do.
Marcus	I don't want to go there. If you want to go out, just pick another place, any place, just not there.
Pam	Forget it. I am going to get a glass a wine.

You might very well be wondering, "What's up with Marcus?" As it turns out that new restaurant is run by one of Marcus' college classmates, the same guy who Marcus' college sweetheart cheated on him with. The experience was very humiliating for Marcus, and he didn't want to share it with Pam. This "outside factor" was clearly impeding Marcus' interest in going to the restaurant, and he was unwilling to reveal what the real issue was.

Recognizing Level-3 Disagreements

Level-3 disagreements tend to exhibit at least one of the following telltale signs, and sometimes all three.

- **There is an unwillingness to share information.** If you partner is not willing to share their thinking or the reasons behind it, there may very likely be an outside factor causing the disagreement.
- **The arguments are irrational.** If you find that the reasons your partner gives for their disagreement don't appear to make sense, or if each time you address a reason they give a new reason, there may be some outside factor causing the disagreement.
- **There is no commitment to finding a solution.** If you partner rejects every solution you come up with, without coming up with one of their own, you may very well be dealing with a level-3 issue.

Solving Level-3 Disagreements

You can't solve level-3 disagreements by focusing on the issue. Why? Because it's not about the issue. You also can't solve level-3 disagreements by discussing strengths and weaknesses. Why? Because it's not about values. Level-3 disagreements require a significantly different approach.

- **Empathize with the position.** It can be quite frustrating when it appears that your partner is being irrational or obstinate. Yet with this principle, it is important to address your partner with care and consideration. If your partner is dealing with an outside factor that is impacting their interaction with you, it can be helpful to remind them how much you care about them and their happiness. In the above disagreement, Pam might say: *Hey, it's important to me that you be happy with where we go for the celebration.*

- **Use observation techniques and reflective listening**. State what you observe and reflect back what you think that might mean. As an example, Pam might say: *At the same time, you are usually ready to try new places. But I hear your words and it feels out of character for you to have such a strong reaction to a restaurant.*

- **Ask for permission to dig deeper.** Pam might continue, *I don't want to assume that something is wrong. I care about you and want to understand. Can we talk about it? If not now, then sometime over the next couple of days?*

- **Listen and affirm.** If your partner does share what the outside factor is, listen and affirm their concern, and seek resolution.

- **Let time pass if necessary.** Of course, sometimes your partner will request that you allow time to pass. When the agreed upon time has passed, if your partner has not brought the issue back up, do so in an affirming way, such as, *It's been a few days since we talked about … It would really help me to know you better and know how to best love you if we can take some time to get clear on what's behind your thoughts and feeling on.… Can we do that now?*

Level-3 disagreements can be the most difficult type to resolve since the disagreement is based on factors that likely have little to do with the alternatives. However, with care, communication, and patience, even the toughest level-3 disagreements can be addressed.

Determining the Disagreement Level

So how do you determine if a disagreement is level-1, level-2 or level-3?

- First, determine if the disagreement is level 3. Recall the criteria. If any one of these exists, it is likely a level-3 disagreement.
    - Is there an unwillingness to share information?
    - Are the arguments irrational?
    - Is there a lack of commitment to finding a solution?

- If you can rule out level-3, then assume it is a level-1 disagreement and build a PAC and ask, *How would that work?* to ensure you both have the same information.

- If building a PAC doesn't resolve the issue, you can be confident that you are dealing with a level-2 disagreement and can use the level-2 resolution strategies.

Proactive Strategies

You can think of the approaches for addressing each of the levels of disagreement as intervention strategies—that is, things to do if a disagreement occurs. Now let's talk about proactive strategies—things you can do to prevent a disagreement from occurring in the first place.

Preventing Level-1 Disagreements.

- Recall that level-1 disagreements are based on a lack of information. You can be proactive in preventing level-1 disagreements by being intentional about providing your partner all the information they may need to better understand the alternative you are proposing.
- If you find that you and your partner frequently have level-1 disagreements, do a debrief occasionally with each other. Ask: "What information could I have said before the disagreement started that would have prevented the disagreement from occurring?"
- You can use this information to inform how you present ideas to your partner in the future.

Preventing Level-2 Disagreements

- Level-2 disagreements are typically based on you and your partner having different values. You can help alleviate level-2 disagreements by being transparent, explicit, and proactive about sharing the values you hold that result in you preferring your alternative. Recall that you can get at values by identifying strengths. So, you might say, for example, "I want to do this because I value ..." and then speak about the strengths of your alternative.

Preventing Level-3 Disagreements

- Since level-3 disagreements are based on personality, past history, or other outside factors, you can be proactive in addressing level-3 disagreements by recognizing your own outside issues that may be impacting your view of the alternatives and being explicit and transparent about them.

In some cases, these proactive strategies can prevent the disagreement from occurring at all. In other cases, they can help resolve the disagreement more quickly and prevent it from becoming a conflict.

Deeper Dive

Our method of addressing conflict often comes from the modeling we saw as children. For example, if disagreement was handled by complete avoidance or by in-your-face confrontation, you may find that your tendency is to do the same. Consider exploring these deeper questions which may help you better understand why your tendencies with conflict are what they are.

- In your family, were people allowed to disagree with one another?
- What type of disagreements (level 1, 2, 3), if any, did you observe in your household, what were the disagreements about, and how were they handled?
- What types of disagreements did you have with others while growing up, and with former romantic partners?
- What were these disagreements about, and how were they handled?

From these questions, do you notice any similarities or differences in how you address disagreement with your partner today?

Summary and Close

The table that follows summarizes the approach to each of the three levels of disagreement.

Level-1 Disagreements: Lack of Shared Information

1	**P**layback what you believe you heard and confirm that you heard it correctly.	*It sounds like you are saying…is that right?*
2	**A**gree with what you can agree with.	*I certainly agree that…*
3	**C**hallenge by asking a question to address your concerns.	*If we do this, how… or How would that work?*

Level-2 Disagreements: Different Values

1	Agree to try to resolve the disagreement using *The Porsha Principles* approach.	*This is an important issue; might we try to apply the Porsha Principles to this?*
2	Identify what you agree on and confirm the source of the disagreement.	*We seem to both agree that…. Where we seem to be disagreeing is…. Is that right?*
3	Confirm the alternatives and ask for others.	*I'm wanting to … and you're wanting to…. Do I have that right? Are there other alternatives we should consider?*
4	Together, define the strengths of each alternative over the other alternatives.	*Let's first talk about the strengths of each alternative …*
5	Together identify the weaknesses of each alternative. (If there are only two alternatives, this step may not be necessary, as the strengths of one alternative will likely be the weakness of the other.)	*Now let's identify the weaknesses of each alternative …*
6	Check for agreement.	*Have the strengths and weaknesses helped us to agree on one of the alternatives?*
7	Have each partner identify the one or two most important strengths of their alternative.	*What do you see as the one or two most important strengths of your alternative?*

8	Seek a merged alternative.	*Can we think of an alternative that combines these key strengths?*

Level-3 Disagreements: Outside Factors

1	Empathize with the position by addressing your partner with care and consideration.	*It's important to me that you be happy with …*
2	Use observation techniques and reflective listening.	*At the same time, you are usually…. But I hear your words and it feels out of character for you to …*
3	Ask for permission to dig deeper.	*I don't want to assume that something is wrong. I care about you and want to understand. Can we talk about it? If not now, then sometime over the next couple of days?*
4	Listen and affirm.	*Thanks for explaining. I certainly can understand …*
5	Let time pass if necessary and bring back up in an affirming way.	*It's been a few days since we talked about…. It would really help me to know you better and to know how to best love you if we can take some time to get clear on what's behind your thoughts and feeling on…. Can we do that now?*

These strategies take practice. You won't be good at them right away, and sometimes, in the heat of a disagreement, you will forget to use them completely. But at any time, even after the disagreement, you can come back and begin again with, "This is an important issue; might we try to apply The Porsha Principles with this?" Refine these strategies and make them your own as you continue to create and sustain your lifelong honeymoon with your partner.

<table>
<tr>
<td>

Practicing the Principle

</td>
<td>

Learning from Past Disagreements

This principle focused on resolving conflict by understanding the three reasons people disagree and providing strategies for addressing each one. To help you and your partner with future disagreements, this exercise has you examining past disagreements and identifying how you would have liked to have handled them.

Take the following steps.

1. Together, identify three to five disagreements that have occurred in the past.

2. With each disagreement decide whether it was level 1 (information), 2 (values), or 3 (outside factors).

3. Discuss the strategy from *The Porsha Principles* that might have been used to better handle each disagreement.

   - Building a PAC
   - Delineation
   - Strengths and weaknesses
   - Merged alternatives
   - Empathizing and digging deeper

4. Finally, decide what "catch phrase" (e.g., "Let's use our Porsha Principles on this") you and partner will use in the future to help remind you to pull in one of the strategies to help with a disagreement.

</td>
</tr>
</table>

Notes

Notes

Principle 7:
Repair Ruptures...They Can Ruin You

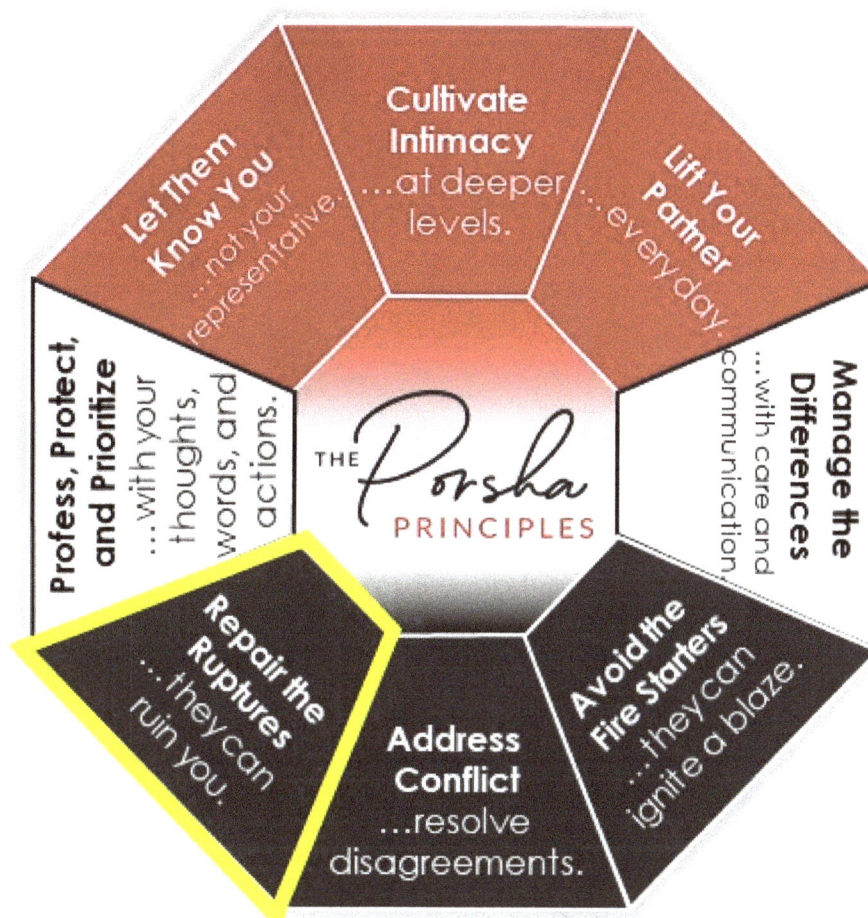

What You Will Learn	**Foundation**
	• What are the three types of relationship ruptures?
	• What is an attachment bond and how does a rupture impact it?
	Proactive Strategies
	• What are the early symptoms of a possible rupture and what action should you take in advance?
	• What are three strategies for preventing ruptures?
	Intervention Strategies
	• What are five steps for addressing a rupture should one occur?
	Action
	• Steps you and your partner can take to put the principle into practice: "Ruptures in Our Relationship"

Introduction

In every relationship, there will be times when the couple will hit a road bump. Some bumps will be small and easily resolved. Others may be ignored for a period until they become much bigger issues. And still others can cause significant damage to the relationship and require more serious and concentrated intervention.

As an example, let's go back to Pam and Marcus and take a look at a conversation in their relationship.

Marcus comes home an hour late after Pam has called him multiple times.

- As soon as he enters the front door, Pam says, *Why haven't you answered your phone?*
- Marcus explains, *I'm sorry, my phone died, and I thought I would just try to get home as soon as I could.*
- Pam is unable to let it go. *I don't believe you. Whenever I can't reach you, you always say it is because your battery has died.*
- Pam reaches for the phone and says, *Let me see your phone.*
- Marcus pulls away and responds, *See, there you go again, you don't trust me. You are trying to control me. You weren't like this when we first got married. It doesn't say a lot for our marriage that you want to check up on me like this.*
- Pam spirals out of control, *You're probably cheating on me again!*
- Marcus shakes his head. *You will never forgive me for that one mistake.*

This kind of spiral can happen frequently in a relationship in which ruptures are not repaired—like a sore that is allowed to fester, it can infect other areas of the relationship, and sometimes even cause the relationship to need major surgery.

As you will see later, this was an innocent situation, as it is many times for couples. Marcus' phone battery did die, and he really was tied up in traffic rushing to get home. So why did this conversation spiral so out of control for the couple?

- First, it is clear from their interaction that the initial rupture (an affair Marcus had three years ago) was never fully repaired through some type of *intervention* strategy.
- Second, not only wasn't a full repair done, no *proactive* strategy was put in place to address possible future triggers.

In this section, I will show you what couples can do to repair a rupture and prevent future ruptures from occurring.

Sound Familiar?

Think about times in your relationship when you have thought or felt, "Here we go again." Take the time to examine what was going on at the time. What was the behavior of your partner that triggered that thought or feeling? It is highly likely that the "here we go again" feeling is related to either a fire starter or an unrepaired rupture.

First, let's talk about adult attachment bonds, which are just a way of describing how we attach to romantic partners. We seek secure attachment bonds in order to feel safe, protected, and loved. According to Dr. Sue Johnson[8], a leading researcher in the science of attachment and bonding, the key to a secure attachment and long-lasting love is emotional responsiveness.

Three Characteristics of Emotional Responsiveness

> **Research shows that marriages fail not due to increasing conflict but decreasing affection and emotional responsiveness.**

What are the three characteristics of emotional responsiveness?

- **Accessibility** – *When I reach for you, can I find you? Are you there when I need you most?* Partners are open and attentive to one another.

- **Responsiveness** – *When I need care, comfort, to be seen or to be heard, do you respond when I need you most?* Partners can rely on the other to engage on an emotional level during the difficult times as well as the good times. This type of connection is very calming to your partner's nervous system and messages them that they are not alone in the world.

- **Engagement** – *Do I feel you value me, are attracted to me, and have my best interests at heart?* This type of connection is also very calming to your partner's nervous system and messages to them that they matter to you.

Note that research[9] shows that marriages fail not due to increasing conflict but decreasing affection and emotional responsiveness.

When ruptures happen they break down a couple's attachment bond. When a bond is threatened, many times partners will exhibit anxious or avoidant behaviors. The attachment bond goes from secure to insecure, creating anxiety

---

[8] Sue Johnson, *Hold Me Tight, Seven Conversations for a Lifetime of Love* (New York: Little, Brown Spark, 2008), 57-58.
[9] Hutson, et al, "The Connubial Crucible: Newlywed Years as Predictors of Marital Delight, Distress, and Divorce." *Journal of Personality and Social Psychology*, 80(2), 237–252.

and disconnection. These symptoms can worsen and cripple the relationship if the rupture isn't repaired.

Three Types of Ruptures

When I speak of ruptures, I am talking about three different types.

The Three Types of Ruptures: Scrapes, Bruises, Deep Cuts

(Keep in mind that we are using these terms as metaphors to describe degrees of emotional hurts. They are not intended to refer to physical wounds.)

- **Scrapes**. Scrapes are simple abrasions caused by differences rubbing against one another. No one is at fault; the scrape is typically caused by a difference.

  For example, when it comes to decision-making Marcus is strongly decisive and makes decisions quickly, while Pam tends to be more deliberate and take more time to make decisions. So, when it comes to eating out, Marcus can find himself becoming quite irritated with Pam over the time it takes for her to not only choose a place, but also to choose what she wants to order. At times this small scrape can feel like a major rupture, especially when he is hungry, or "hangry" as the popular term goes.

- **Bruises**. Bruises occur when one of the partners is at fault and a harm is caused to the other partner. Examples of this might include:
  - Coming home after a stressful day at work and snapping at your partner
  - Forgetting an important date such as a birthday or anniversary
  - Not following through on an agreement made with your partner
  - A verbal attack that is hurtful to your partner

- **Deep Cuts**. Deep cuts, like bruises, occur when one of the partners is at fault and a harm is caused to the other partner. However, the rupture of a deep cut is significantly more severe. The wound is deep and potentially fatal to the relationship. Examples might include:
  - Missing a critical event such as the birth of a child or an occasion where your partner is being awarded or recognized for an accomplishment
  - Spending a large amount of money without consulting your partner
  - Reckless behavior that puts you or your partner in harm's way
  - An affair
  - A physical assault

So how do you prevent ruptures from happening and how should you intervene should one occur? In this principle we want to start first with intervention strategies.

Back to Pam and Marcus

In the earlier scenario, we heard how Marcus not returning Pam's calls triggered her back to the event of Marcus' affair three years before. The trigger signals that this deep cut was likely not fully repaired. So, what was missing? Let's look at what they did at the time of the affair, and then at what should have been done.

What was done three years ago?

- Pam discovered the hotel receipt and confronted Marcus in tears.
- Marcus came clean. He said it was a mistake that just happened once, begged for her forgiveness, and swore it would never happen again.
- Pam was angry and upset for about a week. She eventually decided to forgive him and wanted to put it all behind them as quickly as possible.

This is the proverbial "sweeping it under the rug." Unfortunately, far too often, deep cuts are addressed in just this way. Why does this happen? Partners often address symptoms and not root causes. Therapists understand that if you treat the symptoms of an issue without addressing the fundamental root causes, you could be setting yourself up for a potentially even more devastating outcome later.

As an example, a cheating spouse can be convinced to stop having that affair, but unless the partners address the underlying causes for the affair, a repeat rupture is more likely.

What needed to be done?

Pam and Marcus needed to do two things together: *stabilize* and *strategize*. How do you do this? Take a look at the approach that follows.

The Five Steps for Addressing a Relationship Rupture

To stabilize, the offending party should:
1. Address and fully understand the emotional impact their behavior had on their partner.
2. Express deep remorse, apologize, and take full ownership of their behavior without making excuses or trying to explain the behavior.

To strategize, together they should:
3. Isolate the likely root cause of the behavior.
4. Identify what could have been done to prevent it.
5. Identify where they are now and what will be done differently going forward.

I believe the key to recovering from a rupture is to do the five steps described above as soon as possible and repeat as needed. Deep ruptures are seldom a "one-and-done." They often require several discussions over an extended period of time for full repair.

In the case of Pam and Marcus, their five steps to stabilize and strategize may have looked like the following.

1	**Address and fully understand the emotional impact your behavior had on your partner.** Marcus fully listens without interrupting as Pam describes how his behavior broke her heart and betrayed her trust. She tells him that she felt she was such a fool to have believed him when he said he didn't answer her calls because his phone had died.
2	**Express deep remorse, apologize, and take full ownership of their behavior without making excuses or trying to explain the behavior.** Marcus first acknowledges how his actions resulted in breaking the heart of the one person in the world he is supposed to be protecting and caring for most. He lets her know how ashamed he is for betraying her with the affair and then lying to her to cover it up. He emphasizes that this was 100% his fault and there was nothing she did to deserve this.
3	**Isolate the likely root cause of the behavior.** After much discussion, the couple was able to isolate these likely root causes: • Marcus was feeling neglected emotionally and sexually. He felt Pam had been less attentive to his needs after being promoted to a vice president position and taking on more responsibilities. • Pam agreed that she was being less attentive to Marcus' needs. However, she felt Marcus was being selfish and was not supporting her promotion by giving her time to get adjusted to her new position. • Marcus agreed that he should have been more supportive and had no business going outside the relationship to have his needs met.
4	**Identify what could have been done to prevent it.** They both agreed that Marcus should have come to her and indicated the rupture he was feeling. They could have come to an agreement on how they would secure more time together to ensure both of their needs were met.

5	**Identify where they are now and what will be done differently going forward.**
	Although hopeful, Pam indicated that she would have a hard time trusting Marcus going forward. And, just as happened with the affair, when there are times he doesn't respond to her phone calls she is going to feel scared and insecure. They agree that Marcus will increase his transparency and accessibility by temporarily adding the "Life 360" app to his phone and making sure his phone is charged at all times.

Keep in mind that, depending on the degree of the rupture, it could take minutes or months to repair. In some cases, the couple should seek professional help.

Identifying Causes of Ruptures

The key to preventing a rupture from occurring is to *identify potential causes*, *recognize the early symptoms* that a rupture is likely imminent, and then *take proactive steps* to prevent the rupture from occurring. Let's first take a look at potential causes and those early symptoms of scrapes, bruises, and deep cuts.

Causes of scrapes

Recall that with scrapes, no one is at fault. Instead, the rupture is likely the result of poorly managing a difference.

Potential Causes	Early Symptoms
• Personality differences • Misunderstandings • Miscommunications	• You find yourself irritated by the way your partner does something. • You find yourself arguing over a minor thing. • You find yourself wanting to avoid talking about a topic or bringing up a concern. • You find yourself wanting to spend less time with your partner

Causes of bruises and deep cuts

Bruises are a result of one of you injuring the other, intentionally or unintentionally. Deep cuts, on the other hand, go beyond bruises by causing significant damage to a couple's relationship. Bruises and deep cuts tend to have similar causes and similar early symptoms. The difference is in the impact of the behavior. For some people and some situations, the offending behavior (e.g., an unkind word or not following through on an agreement) will cause a bruise. For other people or other situations, the same behavior will cause a deep cut.

To prevent bruises and deep cuts from occurring it is important to be aware of the early symptoms and take action in advance.

Potential Causes	Early Symptoms
• Stress • Inability to express emotions in a healthy way • Inability to control emotions • Self-absorption and inconsideration	• You find yourself arguing often and more intensely. • What starts out as avoidance begins creeping into resentment of your partner. • You find yourself "walking on eggshells" to avoid causing a blowup. • You find yourself questioning whether you want to be in the relationship.

Any one of these actions can have severe consequences to the stability of your relationship. Therefore, it is important that you take action to prevent these actions from taking place.

Proactive Strategies

If you find yourself experiencing one of the early symptoms described above, consider the following actions.

1. Focus on Porsha Principles 2, 3 and 8 as daily practices in your relationship. These principles help keep you in the mindset of valuing your partner and the relationship.
   - Principle 2: Cultivate intimacy … on deeper levels.
   - Principle 3: Lift your partner … every day.
   - Principle 8: Profess, protect, and prioritize your relationship ... with your thoughts, words, and actions.

2. Hold weekly check-ins with your partner to avoid holding onto hurts until they become ruptures. In those weekly check-ins consider having each partner answer the following questions.
   - What went well this week in our relationship?
   - What were the events in this past week, if any, which felt like a small or big rupture?

3. To prevent a further rupture, and in addressing a rupture, it may be necessary to call a timeout. Take 30 minutes or more to identify what you need and why you were triggered. Be willing to reach for connection again with your partner at an agreed-upon time.

Intervention Strategy

When a rupture-causing event occurs, use the five-step intervention process discussed earlier and presented again below.

Stabilize. To stabilize, the offending party should:

1. Address and fully understand the emotional impact their behavior had on their partner.
2. Express deep remorse, apologize, and take full ownership of their behavior without making excuses or trying to explain the behavior.

Strategize. To strategize, together they should:

3. Isolate the likely root cause of the behavior.
4. Identify what could have been done to prevent it.
5. Identify where they are now and what will be done differently going forward.

Deeper Dive

Many times ruptures can be correlated with early life experiences that we had in our families growing up. Ideally, we would like to come from securely attached families where there is a lot of openness and safety about expressing needs, desires, and ideas. But sometimes we come from families where the environment doesn't support and teach us how to constructively share our thoughts and feelings. Instead, we may internalize feelings like guilt, shame, anger, and rejection, and learn to offload these feelings in unhealthy ways by delivering bruises and deep cuts in our relationships. As a further result, we don't learn to make loving repairs with people we care about.

Consider exploring these deeper questions which may help you better understand why your tendencies are what they are when it comes to creating and repairing ruptures.

- Do you feel it was okay to ask questions and share your feelings with your parents or caregivers?
- What feelings were allowed to be expressed growing up by you or others (e.g., anger, happiness, sadness)?
- How do you deal with feelings of guilt, shame, anger, and rejection? From whom did you learn this?
- What ruptures, if any, did you see your parents or primary caregivers, have in their relationship? To your knowledge, how did they resolve them?
- What does an apology mean to you? Have you ever apologized to someone very important to you? How did it make you feel? Did you notice any changes about you or the relationship afterwards?
- Have you ever refused to give an apology to someone important to you? How did it make you feel? Did you notice any changes about you or the relationship afterwards? What do you wish you had done differently?
- Do you have any unresolved ruptures from past romantic relationships? (If so, you might consider talking with a counselor to help you move past this and heal.)

From these questions, and given your past experiences, do you notice any similarities or differences with how you create and repair ruptures with your partner today?

Summary and Close

Let's recap what we covered in this principle.

- I started out talking about the three types of relationship ruptures and the three keys for preventing relationship ruptures from occurring.

- I identified the early symptoms of a possible rupture and actions you should take in advance.

- I then talked about the five steps for addressing a rupture should one occur.

> **Being proficient at repairing ruptures is a critical element in creating your lifelong honeymoon.**

I consider this principle to be one of the foundations for successful relationships, the bread and butter of Porsha Principles. Ruptures will happen with every couple. It is all about how you respond to the rupture that can make or break the relationship. Being proficient at repairing ruptures is a critical element in creating your lifelong honeymoon.

Practicing the Principle	**Rupture Review**
	This exercise is intended to give you and your partner the opportunity to review a few past ruptures and repair any that are still unhealed. The two of you should take turns answering the following questions.

- For you, what have been the three worst ruptures in our relationship?

- Are there any other ruptures that have not been repaired?

- What can we do to begin repairing each one, if we haven't already?

- What can we do to prevent similar ruptures in the future?

Notes

Notes

Principle 8: Profess, Protect, and Prioritize Your Relationship ... with Your Thoughts, Words, and Actions.

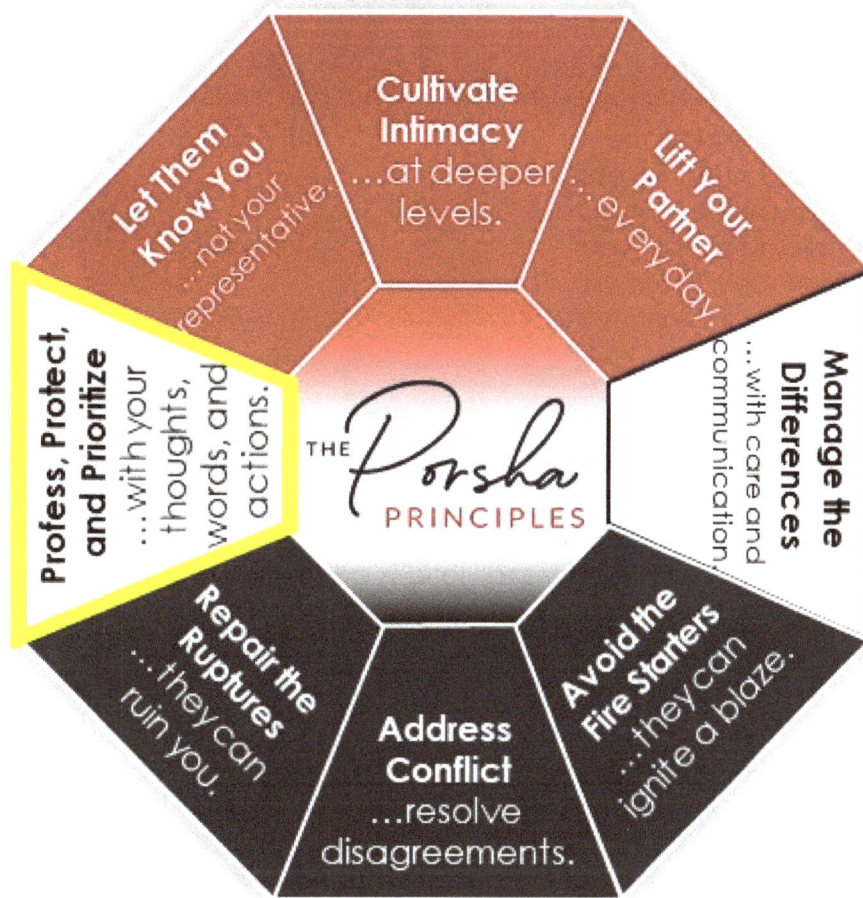

What You Will Learn	**Foundation**
	• Examples of how one can profess, protect, and prioritize the relationship
	Proactive Strategies
	• How boundaries can be used to protect and prioritize the relationship
	• Types of strategies a couple can use to profess, protect and prioritize their relationship
	Intervention Strategies
	• What to do if you feel your partner is not professing, protecting, or prioritizing the relationship
	Action
	• Steps you and your partner can take to put the principle into practice: Our Professing, Protecting, and Prioritizing Plan

Introduction

One of my favorite principles to talk about is, "Profess, protect, and prioritize your relationship … with your thoughts, words, and actions." After you have done the work to lift your partner up, manage the differences, repair ruptures, etc., how do you continue to safeguard your relationship, to sustain your lifelong honeymoon? You must profess, protect, and prioritize the relationship!

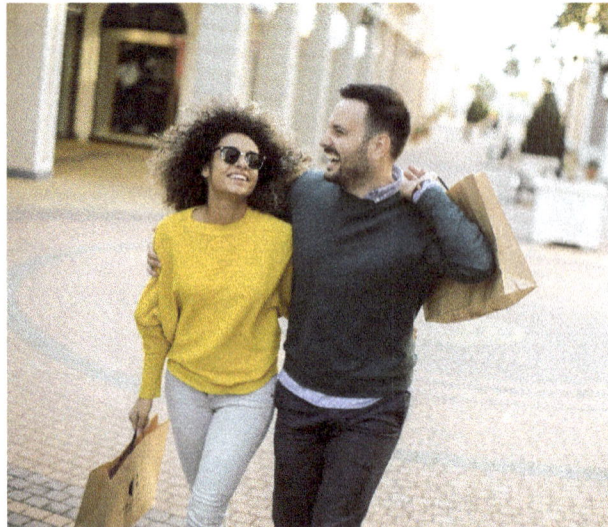

What does this mean? Here are some examples of how Marcus and Pam profess and protect their relationship.

- Marcus frequently **professes** Pam by raving to his friends and family, often with her present, about her promotions and how proud he is of her and the work she does.

- From time to time, Pam is approached by men in her business network for dinner meetings to discuss "business." Pam **protects** the relationship by graciously replying, "Sure, if you don't mind if my husband joins us. Or can you and I can just do coffee instead?"

- Marcus knows that quality time is important to Pam. At the same time, Marcus often gets requests for weekend assignments. To **protect** and **prioritize** their relationship, he and Pam agreed that he would set a healthy boundary at work by not accepting more than one weekend assignment a month.

- Pam frequently **professes** Marcus to her friends and family about the important role he has played in her success by being her strategic thinking partner, helping her to solve difficult work issues.

Revisiting The Power of Thinking

Recall from Principle 3, Lifting your partner … every day that your feelings and behaviors are directly influenced by your thoughts. If you allow your thoughts about your partner to be dominated by negativity, it can begin changing how you feel about your partner and your behavior toward them. To protect your relationship, it's critical that you pay attention to your thinking and be vigilant about eliminating negative thinking.

Of course, if you have an issue with your partner that needs addressing, by all means do so. Use the Porsha Principles to manage the difference, resolve a disagreement, or repair a rupture. Put the intervention strategies to work. However, don't dwell on the dysfunction instead of taking action, and don't lapse into replaying the negative event once the repair has been done.

> **Key: Protect your relationship by protecting your thoughts about your partner.**

The Importance of Boundaries

Boundaries help partners identify what feels good and safe for them in their relationship. They help partners clarify expectations of how to engage with each other and with others. With Marcus and Pam, Marcus had a boundary to not work more than one weekend a month, to protect couple time. Pam had a boundary of not having 1-on-1 business meetings with men after business hours.

Where are boundaries needed? It will depend on the relationship. Here are potential challenge areas where you might consider creating boundaries.

- Disciplining children
- Spending money
- Working hours
- Using social media
- Engaging with family members
- Interacting with former lovers
- Communicating with one another

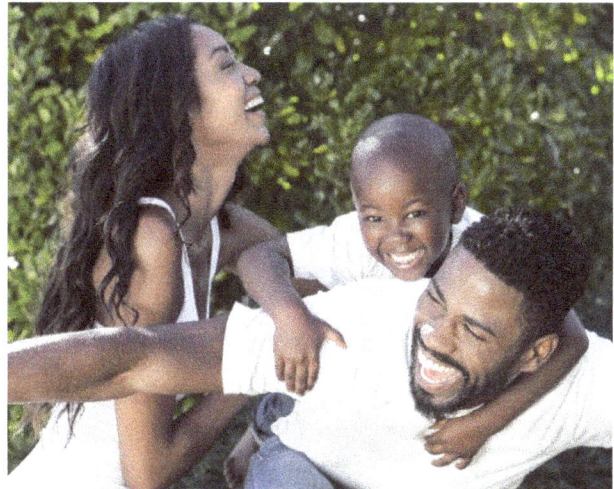

Developing and practicing healthy boundaries will help deepen and strengthen the relationship, leading to your lifelong honeymoon. So, let's look at strategies for professing, protecting and prioritizing your relationship. And then I will talk about what to do if it's not happening.

Deeper Dive

Boundaries are an important piece in protecting a relationship. However, your feelings about boundaries will likely be impacted by your thoughts and experiences with boundaries in the past.

Consider exploring these deeper questions which may help you get to a better understanding of your feelings about boundaries
- What boundaries have you used successfully when it comes to relationships?
- What boundaries have you experienced that were unsuccessful in past relationships?
- How have you felt about setting boundaries with others in the past?
- What are your overall feelings about using boundaries in the future?

From these questions, and given your past experiences, do you notice any similarities or differences with how you address boundaries today?

Transitions

Every couple goes through transitions over the course of their relationship. Couples early in their relationship go through several stages of deepening their closeness. I like the seven stages documented by Julia Paulette Hollenbery.[10]

Transitions in Early Relationships

- Discovery – Passion and excitement, combined with worry over small disappointments
- Hide and seek – The push and pull dance that comes with hopes and fears about whether to explore further
- Imperfection – Increased vulnerability rewarded by acceptance of each other's imperfections
- Trusting – Mutual acceptance continues to build trust.
- Resting – The opening of hearts to real love
- Sharing – The continual renewing that comes from deep sharing of one another
- Intermingling – The full intermingling of one another's lives with a never-ending series of beginnings and endings

Once the intermingling begins and you are in a sustained, committed relationship, transitions continue to occur within the relationship, with children often playing an important role.

Transitions in Sustained, Committed Relationships

- Single and separate
- Single and cohabitating
- Married or other formal commitment
- Infants and adolescents
- Teenagers and young adults
- Empty nesters
- Retirement

However, not only do transitions happen in the relationship, but they also appear outside of the relationship, such as with the following.

Transitions outside the Relationship

- Physical move
- Work promotion or termination
- Caring for sick or elderly loved ones
- Death of a parent or other loved one

---

[10] Julia Paulette Hollenbery, "The 7 Stages of a Loving Relationship," *Happiful Magazine*, December 2021.

Transitions can disrupt relationship patterns and can create new stresses and new needs for you, your partner, or both of you. When transitions happen, it is more important than ever to use your strategies from *The Porsha Principles* to stabilize and strategize as described in Principle 7, Repair the ruptures. In the case of transitions, however, the rupture is caused not by a person but by the transition itself.

Stabilizing and Strategizing with Transitions

To stabilize:

1. Identify and fully understand the emotional impact the transition is having on each of you.
2. Express deep caring and empathy for what your partner is experiencing.

To strategize:

3. Identify the likely impacts of the transition. What will be impacted? What will be different? How will that feel?
4. Brainstorm potential steps you can take to address the impacts.
5. Decide which steps to take and how you will support one another through the transition.

Transitions are seldom easy or simple. Work through them together with much care and consideration for each other.

Proactive Strategies

How you profess, protect, and prioritize **your** relationship will be specific to the two of you and will likely differ from what other couples do for their relationships. However, here is a set of healthy examples that I am offering as a starting point. The key is for you and your partner to discuss what works for you both.

Strategies to Profess Your Relationship

- Vocalize positive thoughts and feelings about your partner.
- Compliment your partner while speaking with others.
- Talk about your partner to others.
- Introduce your partner to your friends and family.
- Stand up for your partner.
- Support your partner's ideas and beliefs.

Strategies to Protect Your Relationship

A key to protecting your relationship is setting healthy boundaries. Below are a few examples based on the area in which a boundary may be needed.

Sample Boundaries to Protect Your Relationship

Area of Need	Sample Boundary
Dealing with family members	We will not talk about problems in our relationship with family members.
Former lovers	We will not initiate contact with any former lovers. If we have any interaction with a former lover, we will inform the other partner.
Disciplining children	We will not say or do anything that undermines the other partner's authority in front of the children.
Communicating with one another	We will call a timeout if one or both of us raise our voices or uses profanity when speaking with the other.
Social media	We will have joint social media accounts; we will avoid following anyone who represents a potential risk to our relationship; we will have guidelines as needed to avoid social media from negatively impacting our time together.
Spending money	We will not spend more than $100 on a discretionary expense without talking with each other in advance unless it is an emergency.
Working hours	We will not do work, including having calls or responding to emails, between 6 and 8 pm each evening, unless it is an emergency or is discussed with the partner ahead of time.

Other Protection Strategies

- Be cautious about using words that might be misinterpreted by another person as indicating interest.
- Pay attention to your negative thoughts about your partner; remember, they influence your feelings and behaviors.
- Avoid such things as fantasizing about past relationships.
- Remove photos or mementos of previous relationships that would bring up memories of the past.
- Address your individual issues that can negatively impact a relationship—such as addictions, anxiety, depression, or other mental health issues. For example, if you suffer from depression, you may not want to do anything or be around other people. This can result in your partner feeling alone or unfulfilled.

- If you and your partner share a spiritual foundation, practice spirituality in your relationship by uplifting each other in prayer and looking for guidance from a higher power.
- Share experiences with your partner. When couples stop sharing experiences it can leave room for sharing those experiences with other people.
- Do things that your partner needs to feel loved but may not come naturally or are less enjoyable to you.
- Actively repair ruptures and proactively prevent them from happening.

Strategies to Prioritize Your Relationship

- Relax and unwind; take some time to focus on each other in a beautiful location.
- Create a bucket list of experiences you want to have together.
- Restate your acceptance of each other and your commitment to the relationship; this allows each of you to be who you are and to do the relationship work in a safe and supportive way.
- Hold a vow renewal in celebration of your love and dedication to one another.
- Take quarterly excursions to have time away alone with each other.
- Hold weekly date nights to maintain a regular romantic connection.
- Consider a couple's retreat to continue to build skills in sustaining healthy, positive interaction with one another.
- Find new fun things to do together to add variety and keep things exciting.
- Monitor how your partner is evolving by regularly checking in on changes to your partner's dreams, and to identify new interests and likes.

Practice these prioritizing strategies as a way to continue to cultivate intimacy and strengthen your attachment bond throughout your lifelong honeymoon.

Intervention Strategies

Ideally we would want to be proactive in the way that we protect, protect, and prioritize our relationships. But when real life kicks in, it's important to be equipped with intervention strategies to get back on track.

1. **Don't be quiet.** When you feel a boundary has been violated, avoid being the silent martyr. Use assertive communication skills to bring up and address the issue, as described in Principle 4, Managing the differences:
   - Use I-statements.
   - Use feeling words.
   - Ask specifically for what you need.

2. **Be emotionally responsive.** Regardless of the degree of a rupture, if your partner is negatively impacted by an interaction with you or an action by you, you must be emotionally responsive by being accessible and emotionally comforting. Validate your partner's feelings, and make sure the rupture is repaired before you and your partner move on.

3. **Take responsibility.** Recall that some ruptures are scrapes—that is, simply caused by a difference, and no one is at fault. But if the rupture is a bruise or deep cut in which one of you is indeed at fault, part of the repair requires the offending partner to take responsibility as soon as possible for their actions. Apologize, and continue to take the required steps to repair the rupture as described in Principle 7: Repair the ruptures.

4. **Be aware of differing interpretations.** Recognize that a bruise for one partner may, for the offending partner, be thought of as a minor scrape. For example, one person may feel that their partner is responsible for creating a bruise or deep cut and should apologize. However, the offending partner may feel it is a minor scrape and that their partner is being "too sensitive" or "overreacting." If the issue is just a matter of differences, it is important for both partners to recognize the difference and work out a solution for the future, versus creating a deeper rupture by arguing over who is at fault and who isn't.

Summary and Close

Let's recap what we have covered in this principle: Profess, protect, and prioritize your relationship ... with your thoughts, words, and actions.

- We opened with looking at ways Pam and Marcus profess, protect, and prioritize their relationship.
- We then revisited the power of thinking and how your feelings and behaviors are directly influenced by your thinking. Therefore, to live your lifelong honeymoon, it is important that you strive to maintain positive thoughts about your partner, always.
- We focused on transitions and the importance of using the stabilizing and strategizing approaches described in Principle 7 to identify changes and how to adapt to them.
- A key to protecting the relationship is to develop and practice healthy boundaries concerning how you will engage with others and each other. We talked about the types of boundaries that might be needed and provided samples.
- We discussed six strategies for professing the relationship, nine strategies for protecting the relationship, and nine strategies for prioritizing the relationship.
- While ideally you will want to be proactive in professing, protecting, and prioritizing your relationship, we also talked about four intervention strategies to use as needed.

Key: Protect your relationship by protecting your thoughts about your partner.

By professing, protecting, and prioritizing your relationship, you are showing your partner that they matter to you, and that the relationship matters to you as well. This is another critical step in creating and sustaining your lifelong honeymoon. It all starts with your thoughts.

Practicing the Principle	**Professing, Protecting, Prioritizing Checkup**
	To put this principle into practice, develop strategies the two of you will use to profess, protect, and prioritize the relationship. To help in this, take turns asking each other the following questions.
	1. **Profess.** What are ways that you have seen me profess you to others? What are one or two other ways you would like for me to profess you?
	2. **Protect.** What are boundaries you have seen me set to protect our relationship? What are one or two other boundaries you would want me to consider?
	3. **Prioritize.** What are things you have seen me do to prioritize our relationship? What are one or two other things you would want me to consider doing to give priority to our relationship?
	After each of you have answered the questions, have each partner indicate which strategies they will commit to implementing. The strategies do not have to be the same for each partner. Document these and make them part of your regular review.

Notes

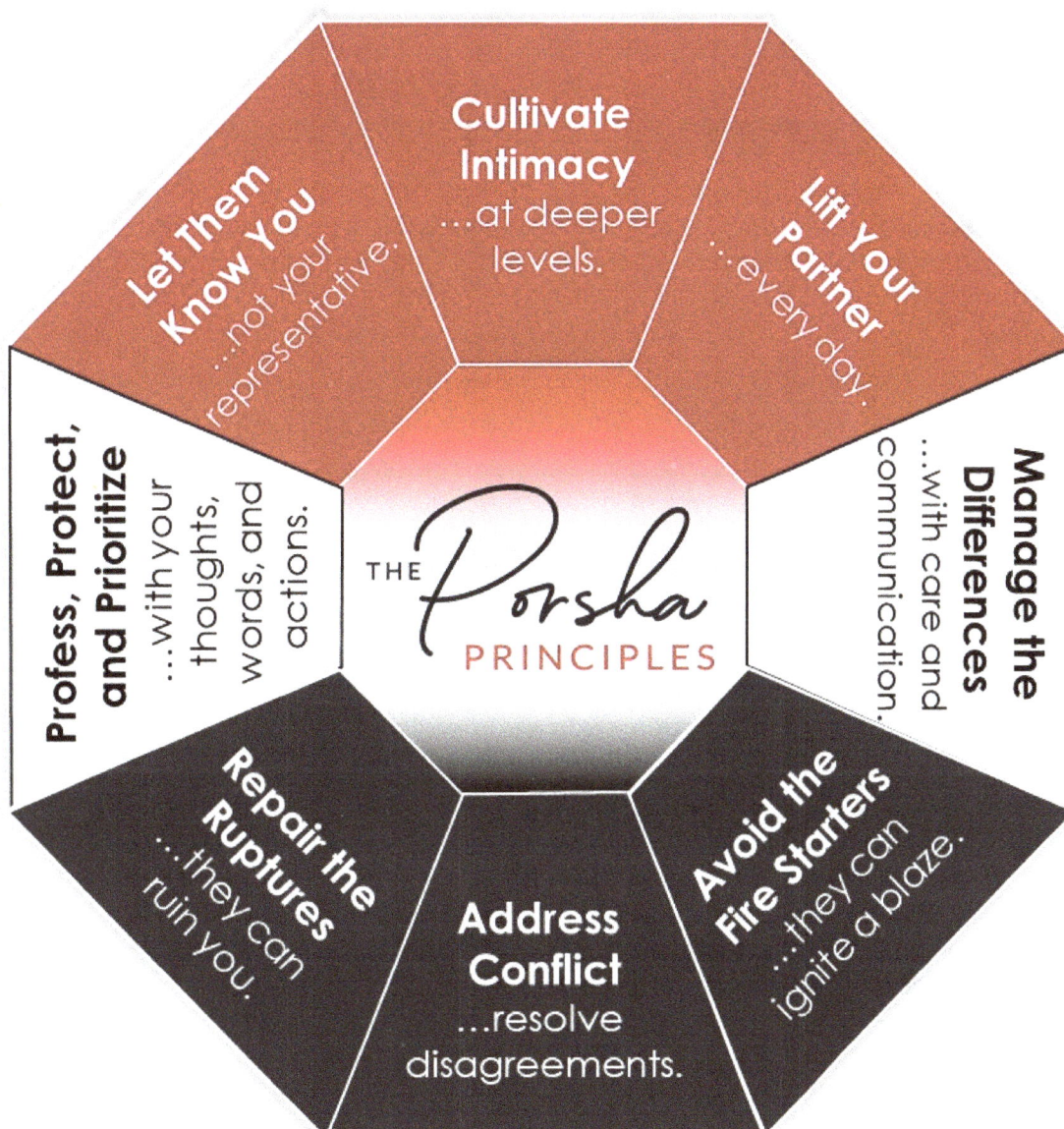

Cultivate Intimacy
...at deeper levels.

Let Them Know You
...not your representative.

Lift Your Partner
...every day.

Profess, Protect, and Prioritize
...with your thoughts, words, and actions.

Manage the Differences
...with care and communication.

THE Porsha PRINCIPLES

Repair the Ruptures
...they can ruin you.

Address Conflict
...resolve disagreements.

Avoid the Fire Starters
...they can ignite a blaze.

Congratulations on completing *The Porsha Principles*! My hope is that as you have gone through the book, you and your partner have been putting the principles into practice. Now it's time to build your action plan for creating and sustaining your lifelong honeymoon.

As I indicated in the Overview, this is not a "one and done" process. You don't get better at playing tennis by reading a book on tennis. Likewise, your relationship won't suddenly be better because you have finished *The Porsha Principles*. Instead, you have to consistently practice the principles, get and give feedback, and practice some more.

I want to recommend that you and your partner map out the first time you will perform each action in the action plan on the next page. In addition, you should determine how frequently you will repeat each step. As I said, this is NOT a one-and-done process. To sustain your lifelong honeymoon requires ongoing care and communication. I have added a suggested frequency, but the choice is up to you.

No matter where you are in your relationship, whether you're dating, newlyweds, or have been at it for a decade or more, you can always reset your relationship, starting with Principle #1: Let them know you, not your representative.

Even when it feels hopeless, or that you will never get out of the negative cycle, or that your differences will always be a problem, you can reset.

- Start with reminding yourself about the positives in the relationship. Think back to your actual honeymoon or other times when the love pool was overflowing between you.

- Then apply the appropriate Porsha Principles with intention and effort to re-establish loving and healthy patterns.

While there may be setbacks where you find yourselves experiencing thoughts, feelings, and interactions from the past, know with confidence that if you desire and are willing to put forth the effort, you can indeed have the lifelong honeymoon that every relationship deserves.

It's through working with the principles that you and your partner will stay on the path to creating and sustaining your lifelong honeymoon together.

> **Key: You and your partner deserve a lifelong honeymoon.
> Do what you have to do to make it work for you!**

Couple's Action Plan

Action	1st Time	Frequency
1. **Complete** the Principles Assessment (online or written).		(Annual)
2. **Determine** your *Principle for Focus* during the month or quarter by reviewing the assessment to identify the areas needing greatest attention.		(Quarterly or Monthly)
3. **Review** the *Principle for Focus* content, either by rereading the book section, reviewing the appropriate video, attending the webinar, etc.		(Quarterly or Monthly)
4. **Do** the *Principle in Practice* together.		(Quarterly or Monthly)
5. **Discuss, decide, and document** the specific actions each of you will take to make that principle a stronger part of your relationship; use the information from steps 3 and 4 to help.		(Quarterly or Monthly)
6. **Take action**: Perform the specific actions you chose.		(Ongoing)
7. **Check in** together on how each of you is doing, how taking action is feeling, and what adjustments to make along the way.		(Monthly or Weekly)
8. **Celebrate** your successes! When you or your partner successfully uses a strategy, point it out, focus on it, celebrate it, make a big deal of it. Look for things to celebrate.		(Weekly or Daily)
9. **Learn and restart**: After celebrating successes, determine what you learned and what you will want to do differently with the next principle, and restart again with step 2.		(Quarterly or Monthly)

Warning: Don't undertake too much. Don't make it a burden. Don't make it a test. If this is not feeling like fun, or if it is not improving your relationship, it simply means that *The Porsha Principles* may not be the right approach for you, or you may be applying them in a way that is not working for one or both of you. Always remember: you and your partner deserve a lifelong honeymoon. Do what you have to do to make it work for you!

Personal Insight	**Are We Living Our Lifelong Honeymoon?** People often ask Michael and me if we actually are living a lifelong honeymoon in our relationship. We reply with a resounding, "Yes!" This is real; we are really living it. We met at a later stage in life and brought with us the maturity, life experiences, and the knowledge we had gained from our own careers helping individuals, couples, and groups to be successful. We had the strong desire to make it work and we had the skills and strategies for success that we have shared with you. We even joked, that "If we can't make this work, maybe nobody can!" Of course there are moments in our relationship when one or both of us forgets or violates a principle. But it never takes long for us to remember, reset, and implement the type of intervention strategies we have shared with you to manage our own differences or even repair a rupture. And every time it happens, we find ourselves in an even more loving space—feeling heard, validated, supported, and most importantly, loved. As the minister says, it works if you work it.

Our Wish for You

At the Porsha Principles organization we are dedicated to helping couples create and sustain their lifelong honeymoon. Nearly everyone wants a satisfying and fulfilling relationship. Yet life seems to bring many issues and bumps in the road that can cause what was once a promising love to turn into a relationship filled with stress, irritation, and disappointment. This doesn't have to be the case.

Our wish for you and your partner is that *The Porsha Principles* gives you the tools and strategies you need to weather just about any storm, so you can have the satisfying and fulfilling relationship you both deserve.

Now that you have read the book, consider deepening your understanding and application of the Porsha Principles.

- If you prefer the VISUAL, consider our **video series**. In these nine videos, you will hear me and Michael cover the material in the book, while providing you visual content that drives home the points.

- If you prefer an EXPERIENCE, sign-up for our next **one-day virtual workshop** or **in-person weekend retreat**. Michael and I together lead these highly interactive sessions that include activities that get you and your partner practicing the Porsha Principles in your relationship.

Here's to your high satisfaction and never-ending thrills as you create and sustain **your** lifelong honeymoon!

Porsha and Michael

Appendix

Appendix I. The Style Comparison Tables

The ten Style Comparison Tables that follow compare each unique DISC combination, starting with a couple where both partners have high-D as their dominant style. Shaded areas in each table represent areas of similarity between the styles.

Table 1: High-D / High-D

- If both partners are high-Ds, they will likely both share characteristics such as decisive, proactive, risk-taking, and outcome-focused.
- However, while they will likely accomplish a lot as a couple, they might have problems with each one making decisions on their own without collaboration or taking the needs of the other into account.

D	D
Decisive	
Proactive	
Risk-taking	
Conflict-resolving	
Objective	
Outcome-focused	
Questioning	
Time scheduled	

Table 2: High-D / High-I

- As you can see, they are similar in the gray areas: decisive, proactive, risk-taking, and conflict-resolving.
- However, they differ in the four other areas. These differences, if not managed well, could lead to significant abrasions in the relationship.
- In particular, with the high-D focused on outcomes, and the high-I focused on relationships, they might have considerable issues when a decision has to been made that includes trade-offs between achieving a desired result and negatively impacting others.

D	I
Decisive	
Proactive	
Risk-taking	
Conflict-resolving	
Objective	Subjective
Outcome-focused	Relationship-focused
Questioning	Accepting
Time scheduled	Time flexible

Table 3: High-D / High-S	D	S
• The high-D / high-S is one of the two couple combinations that can be highly complementary or highly conflicting depending upon whether the two people can respect and honor the differences. • These two styles are different on every one of the dimensions, and this can lead to high levels of conflict in a variety of areas. • However, if they can value the different perspectives, they can leverage the differences in a highly positive way. As an example, in terms of decision-making, if they recognize that the high-D is able to be decisive and the high-S deliberate, they can use the strength of one or the other depending upon what type of decision is needed in a given situation.	Decisive	Deliberate
	Proactive	Reactive
	Risk-taking	Risk-avoiding
	Conflict-resolving	Conflict-avoiding
	Objective	Subjective
	Outcome-focused	Relationship-focused
	Questioning	Accepting
	Time scheduled	Time flexible

Table 4: High-D / High-C	D	C
• As you can see, they are similar in the gray areas: objective, outcome-focused, questioning, and time scheduled. • However, they differ in the four other areas. These differences, if not managed well, could lead to significant abrasions in the relationship. • As an example, when it comes to risk, the high-C will naturally want to avoid taking any unnecessary risks, while the high-D will be more ready to take risks when they perceive the potential reward makes it worth it. This difference in perspective can show up at unpredictable times and can be troublesome if not handled well.	Decisive	Deliberate
	Proactive	Reactive
	Risk-taking	Risk-avoiding
	Conflict-resolving	Conflict-avoiding
	Objective	
	Outcome-focused	
	Questioning	
	Time scheduled	

Table 5: High-I / High-I	I	I
• If both partners are high-Is, they would likely both share characteristics such risk-taking, conflict-resolving, relationship-focused, and accepting. • However, while a high-I couple would likely have a lot of fun together, they might have trouble getting things completed, or overlook details.	Decisive	
	Proactive	
	Risk-taking	
	Conflict-resolving	
	Subjective	
	Relationship-focused	
	Accepting	
	Time flexible	

Table 6: High-I / High-S	I	S
• As you can see, they are similar in the gray areas: subjective, relationship-focused, accepting, and time flexible. • However, they differ in the four other areas. These differences, if not managed well, could lead to significant abrasions in the relationship. • As an example, when it comes to conflict, while the high-S will likely want to avoid any conflict, the high-I will be apt to want to talk about it and talk about it *now*.	Decisive	Deliberate
	Proactive	Reactive
	Risk-taking	Risk-avoiding
	Conflict-resolving	Conflict-avoiding
	Subjective	
	Relationship-focused	
	Accepting	
	Time flexible	

Table 7: High-I / High-C

- Like the high-D / high-S match, the high-C / high-I couple combination can be highly complementary or highly conflicting, depending upon whether the two people can respect and honor the differences.
- These two styles are different on every one of the dimensions, and this can lead to high levels of conflict in a variety of areas.
- However, if they are able to value the different perspectives, they can leverage the differences in a highly positive way. As an example, in terms of focus, if they recognize that the high-C will tend to bring an objective view to most situations while the high-I will be more likely to see key subjective elements, they can use each other's strengths to have a full view of various situations.

I	C
Decisive	Deliberate
Proactive	Reactive
Risk-taking	Risk-avoiding
Conflict-resolving	Conflict-avoiding
Subjective	Objective
Relationship-focused	Outcome-focused
Accepting	Questioning
Time flexible	Time scheduled

Table 8: High-S / High-S

- If both partners are high-Ss, they would likely both share characteristics such as deliberate, reactive, risk-avoiding, and conflict-avoiding.
- A high-S couple are highly likely to have strong bonds and be very supportive of one another. However, they might struggle in dealing with conflict or other issues in their relationship.

S	S
Deliberate	
Reactive	
Risk-avoiding	
Conflict-avoiding	
Subjective	
Relationship-focused	
Accepting	
Time flexible	

	S	C
Table 9: High-S / High-C		
	Deliberate	
	Reactive	
	Risk-avoiding	
	Conflict-avoiding	
	Subjective	Objective
	Relationship-focused	Outcome-focused
	Accepting	Questioning
	Time flexible	Time scheduled

Table 9: High-S / High-C

- As you can see, they are similar in the gray areas: deliberate, reactive, risk-avoiding, and conflict-avoiding.
- However, they differ in the four other areas. These differences, if not managed well, could lead to significant abrasions in the relationship.
- As an example, when it comes to their use of time, a high-C will likely want to plan out their time together and arrive on time for most activities. The high-S, however, will most likely tend to want a more flexible schedule and have little concern about arriving on time.

C	C
Table 10: High-C / High-C	
Deliberate	
Reactive	
Risk-avoiding	
Conflict-avoiding	
Objective	
Outcome-focused	
Questioning	
Time scheduled	

Table 10: High-C / High-C

- If both partners are high-Cs, they would likely both share characteristics such as being objective, risk-avoiding, and outcome-focused
- A high-C couple are highly likely to appreciate one another's tendency to take a logical and analytic approach to life and for being realistic about the future and possibilities.
- However, as a couple, they may struggle with talking about feelings and dealing with relationship issues.

Appendix II. Summary of Proactive and Intervention Strategies

Principle 1: Let them know you…not your representative.

Proactive Strategies

How do you prevent the representative from showing up? Below are five strategies that you can use.

1. Take a first step toward practicing authenticity: challenge yourself to share something real about yourself with your partner that you haven't shared before.

2. Strive to be open and honest with your partner on a regular basis about your deepest thoughts and feelings. Tell your partner about your hopes, fears, dreams, and concerns.

3. As you evolve, let your partner know how you have grown and changed as a person. Let them know your new needs and how they can support you.

4. Do the "Parts of Me" exercise with your partner that appears at the end of this section to uncover and reveal the many parts of yourself.

5. Determine if you are truly ready to love.

   - Many of us have the habit of dating the "same person" over and over again—the names change but the result is always the same. This often happens because we haven't recognized our own unhealthy relationship patterns and haven't developed new ones.

   - Talk this out with safe friends who really know you and know your hang-ups and strengths.

   - If necessary, seek therapy to identify and resolve unhealthy relationship patterns.

Intervention Strategies

What should you do if you catch yourself "representing"?

- Immediately acknowledge it, take responsibility, and reset.
  - *I'm sorry, that's not what I really meant to say.… Let me be completely honest here…*

- Dig deeper and be brave. Share your real feelings and insecurities with you partner.
  - *What I am really feeling is …*
  - *What is hard for me to say is …*

- Ask specifically for what you want.
  - *It would be helpful to me if you would …*

What should you do if you catch your partner "representing"?

- Immediately acknowledge it and request a reset.
    - *I hear your words. But from the way you ... it seems like something else may be going on here. Would you take a second and consider if there is something else you really want to say?*
- Use your assertive communication and reflective listening skills to help your partner express their authentic thoughts and feelings. In Principle 4, Managing the differences, we describe the assertive communication and reflective listening approaches, as summarized below.
    - Use reflective listening to play back what you heard or saw.
        - *It sounds like what you are saying is ...*
    - Use I-statements with feeling words.
        - *When you are holding back and not sharing, I feel ...*
    - Ask specifically for what you need.
        - *It would be helpful to me if you would ...*

Once your partner takes a step toward practicing authenticity with you, make sure you respond with emotional responsiveness. Below are a few examples:

- Make your partner feel heard by using reflective listening to restate what you heard.
- Validate their fears.
    - *I can see why you feel that way.*
- Acknowledge their vulnerability with compassion and empathy.
    - Express comforting words
    - Hug your partner
- Get curious by asking follow-up questions.
    - *Can you tell me more about that?*

Principle 2: Cultivate intimacy...at deeper levels.

Proactive Strategies

Regardless of the intimacy area, what are things that you can do right away to deepen the level of intimacy in your relationship? I want to suggest five strategies in particular.

1. **Daily seeking.** Make daily time for you and you partner to check in with one another at an intimate level. Make sure the conversation goes beyond, "How was your day?" Seek to understand your partner's present dreams, desires, and wishes, and learn how to increase your support for them. Here are questions you may find helpful to move the conversation to a deeper level of intimacy.
    - What are your hopes and dreams for your future?
    - How can I help support you in them?

- What's been on your mind today?
- How did that make you feel?
- Why is that important to you?
- What did you take away from...?
- What do you wish you had done about...?

2. **Proactive sharing**. Be proactive in disclosing your own thoughts and feelings. As examples:

   - When your partner does something that you like, go beyond "Thank you," or "That was nice." Be specific about what you liked and why you liked it. This additional information deepens intimacy and your partner's knowledge of what's important to you and why.

     Example

     I really liked it when you brought flowers today. It makes me know that you think about me even when we are apart.

   - When your partner does something that you don't like, don't ignore the behavior or stop at, "I didn't like that." Instead, let your partner know how it made you feel and why.

     Example

     You promised that you would make time for you and me tonight, but you spent two hours talking with your girlfriends on the phone about your day. That makes me feel sad because your actions say to me that my desires are not that important to you.

   - If you have been churning on something and you realize you have been keeping it to yourself, don't continue churning. Instead, turn to your partner and share what's been on your mind.

     Example

     Hey, I may have seemed a bit distracted lately. There's something that's been bothering me that I want to share with you because I can use your help in thinking it through.

3. **Supportive response**. When your partner does share an intimate thought, a supportive response is often necessary to promote further deepening of your intimacy.

4. **Connection rituals**. Be intentional about making memories by creating rituals of connection to increase your level of trust, reliance, and predictability with each other. With higher levels of trust, you and your partner will likely feel more comfortable with going to deeper levels of intimacy. Your connection rituals might include activities such as the following.

   - Morning coffee time
   - Mid-day "thinking of you" texts
   - Occasional special sex dates
   - Weekly date night out
   - Working on a scrap book documenting your travels

- Holiday trips
- "Cuddle quickies"

5. **Intentional acts of love**. Recognize what makes your partner feel close to you and give that gift to them as a way of deepening intimacy. For example, for your partner the key might be praising them, touching them, giving something to them, doing something for them, or just spending time with them. Whatever it is for your partner, be intentional about giving them what they need to feel close. (When we talk about lifting your partner in Principle 3, we will more thoroughly discuss love languages and how to ensure your partner is feeling loved.)

Intervention Strategies

While the proactive strategies are things you can do in advance to establish a pattern of healthy intimacy, intervention strategies may be necessary should intimacy break down or when there is a rupture that needs repair. I want to focus on three strategies in particular that align with times when you or your partner is not sharing, not seeking, or not supporting.

1. **Not Sharing: When your partner doesn't want to engage**
   What do you do if your partner often appears distant or refuses to have a conversation at anything other than a surface level?

   - Use your healthy communication skills to let your partner know how important it is to you that you really know them, and how it makes you feel shut out and alone when they don't share their thoughts and feelings.

     <u>Example</u>

     It is important to me that I really know you. I feel shut out and alone when you ignore me and don't share what you're thinking.

   - When they know that you are hurting, rather than just complaining about their behavior, there is a much higher probability that they will turn toward you and become open to sharing.

2. **Not Seeking: If your partner doesn't seek to know you**
   If your partner doesn't ask questions about you or seems to lose interest when you are sharing about yourself.

   - Let your partner know about your observation and how it makes you feel.

     <u>Example</u>

     It seems that you don't ask questions about me and at times when I am sharing about me, you seem to lose interest or change the conversation back to you. I suspect you don't mean to do it, but it leaves me feeling unimportant and that you are not that interested in knowing me and how I feel about things. And I need you to do this for me to feel close to you.

3. **Not Supporting: If you or your partner becomes critical**
   - If YOU become critical, here is an action to consider.

- As you will learn in Principle 5, Avoid the fire starters, criticism is a fire starter that often leads to feelings of disconnection with your partner.
- Backtrack and quickly apologize.

Example

I am sorry. That sounded so critical and that's not what I meant. What I want to say instead is ..." or "I'm so sorry, can I start over?"

- If YOUR PARTNER becomes critical:
  - Let your partner know in the moment that what they said felt critical. Ask them if they could restate their message in a softer tone.

Example

Hey, please stop. I am feeling criticized when you talk that way and in that tone. Can you say what you want to say in a different way and in a softer tone?

Principle 3: Lift your partner...every day.

Proactive Strategies

1. **Start with your own thinking.**

   If you are not feeling the desire to love your partner in the way they want to be loved, or if you are feeling that the sparks seem to be dying out, start with your own thinking.

   - Nurture your fondness and admiration for your partner by such activities as:
     - Regularly reminding yourself of your partner's most positive qualities
     - Saving memories, such as pictures, letters, and other items
     - Seeking to focus on positive aspects of your partner anytime you find yourself thinking negatively about them
   - Pay close attention to how you are thinking about your partner throughout the day. When you catch yourself focused on a negative, take a minute to nurture fondness and admiration for your partner as described above.

2. **Cultivate in yourself the desire to fulfill your partner's needs.**

   Most of us are wired to look out for self first and to focus on ensuring our own needs are met. So how do you get yourself to focus on fulfilling your partner's needs?

   - Remind yourself that you love your partner and that they are the most important person in the world to you, and that contributing to their happiness is one of your highest priorities.
   - Visualize yourself taking an action that brings joy to your partner and feel the joy inside yourself when you visualize the joy on their face.

3. **Learn your partner's love language.**

   Use the love language test (https://www.5lovelanguages.com/quizzes/love-language) or the magic love language question to learn your partner's love language.

4. **Identify your own internal barriers.**

   Identify any barriers in you that may hinder your expressing love in your partner's love language. Don't be surprised if you find yourself reluctant, challenged, judgmental, or even resentful about having to adjust your actions to meet your partner's love language. Examples:

   - For a partner who did not grow up with affection through physical touch, they may feel challenged by meeting the physical touch needs of their partner because it may feel awkward to them, or they may just not be used to it.

   - A person who has gifts as their primary love language may be judged as materialistic by their partner whose primary love language is touch or acts of service.

   - Gender-specific beliefs can also be barriers. For example, a woman may feel her partner is "weak" if he needs words of affirmation to feel loved. Likewise, a man whose partner needs acts of service to feel loved may feel it's not a "manly" thing to do to help out with "woman's" work around the house.

   To overcome barriers such as these, it is always important to go back to key strategy #1: Remember that you love your partner and want your partner to feel loved. I will discuss in Principle 4, Managing the differences, things you can do to address these barriers to lifting your partner, including dispelling negative beliefs, removing judgment and criticism, and becoming more open to loving your partner differently.

5. **Learn multiple ways to express your love in your partner's love language.**

   Knowing your partner's love language is not enough. It is essential to your lifelong honeymoon that you lift your partner every day by learning to love them the way they want to be loved. It's the small, daily acts of thoughtfulness and attention that breed intimacy and friendship. However, this can be challenging if their love language is different from yours. So, what are strategies you might use? Here are just a few strategies for showing love to your partner.

   - Words of affirmation
     - Keep a running list (mental or physical) of all the positive things your partner does, so you have them ready for use!
     - Daily leave little complimentary notes for your partner.
     - Vocalize positive thoughts and feelings about your partner in their presence and in the presence of others.
     - Write love letters or poems to your partner about how special they are to you.

- Acts of service
    - Give your partner a day off their chores and you fill in!
    - When you see your partner has a need, don't wait until they ask for help; instead initiate helping them.
    - Ask your partner to create a list of things that they would love for you to do.
    - Pay someone to come in and finish a project of your partner's choosing.
- Receiving Gifts
    - Gift your partner with their favorite things often. For example, if they like flowers, maybe subscribe to a flower club so your partner will receive this gift like clockwork!
    - Keep a notebook about the little things that your partner makes comments on; they can make perfect gifts!
    - Get creative and give your partner a coupon book full of gifts (e.g., electronic device, necklace, pair of shoes) that they can redeem whenever they like.
    - Instead of a coupon book of gifts, make the coupons various personal actions such as "good for an evening out," "good for a foot massage," or "good for taking care of a chore."
- Quality time
    - Discuss the top five things you like to do as a couple and make regular plans to do them together.
    - Surprise your partner with a babysitter and take them out for a kid-free night on the town.
    - Carve out daily "sacred space" for 30 minutes to give your partner your undivided attention.
    - Plan a surprise lunch date.
- Physical touch
    - Greet your partner with hugs and kisses regularly.
    - Let your partner know you desire them with a sexual touch.
    - At random times when you are together reach out and stroke/caress your partner.
    - Plan a sexy evening for your partner.

Be creative with your approach to your partner's love language, but everything in moderation. Avoid using the same approach every time. For example, If your partner likes physical touch, don't touch them the same way every time. Strive to be creative!

6. **Don't major in the minors.**
    - Recognize that for most of us, the tendency is to focus on loving our partner the way we want to be loved. I call that majoring in the minors because these things might not be important to your partner at all.

- Instead, major in the majors by focusing on the things important to your partner, not the things you think should be important to them.

7. **Seek feedback from you partner on how much your actions make them feel loved.**

   - Consider doing a modified version of what Gary Chapman calls "The Tank Check." Check weekly or monthly with your partner and ask, "On a scale of 1-to-10, how much have you been feeling loved by me over this past week?" If your partner's tank is below a 7 or 8, ask, "What can I do right now to begin refilling your tank?" While this may sound unromantic or artificial, feedback is critical to creating your lifelong honeymoon. You don't want to have long periods lacking fulfillment, which drain your love pool.

8. **Do a self-check.**

   - Adapting to another person's style is not always easy or comfortable. Therefore, it's important to be emotionally honest with yourself as you practice loving your partner in their love language. From time to time, do a self-check on how this is feeling for you. Ask yourself:
     - How does it make me feel when I am loving my partner in their love language?
     - Do I like the feeling? Why or why not?
     - If you don't like the feeling, talk about your discomfort with your partner and the things you both can do to support you.

Intervention Strategies

What should you do when YOU are not feeling loved?

Find a time to give your partner feedback. If it feels too hard to say it, write a letter to your partner. Below is a helpful approach for you to consider.

1. Start with positivity.

   I know you love me and that my feeling loved is important to you.

2. State your intention by sharing how you are feeling and how important it is to you to bring about a change.

   I know that over the past several weeks I haven't felt that love from you, and I want to see what we can do to address that.

3. Make your request.

   You know that my primary love language is quality time, and I have been really missing it and missing you. One of the things I think can help is if we can make a priority to have dinner together at least five times each week. That way I will know that I will get quality time with you regularly.

   Can you make sure you are home by 6:00 pm on the nights that we commit to eat dinner together?

4. Get input.

   How do you feel about this suggestion?

5. Seek alternatives if necessary.

   Do you have a different suggestion?

6. Confirm agreement.

   So, we are in agreement then that we will...

7. Have a monitoring process.

   Interventions often are needed to correct an unhelpful pattern. But, without a monitoring process, the unhelpful pattern can set in again. Therefore, have a periodic check-in process to ensure that you continue to love one another the way each of you need to be loved.

What to do when YOUR PARTNER tells you they are not feeling loved by you?

1. Let them know you heard them by restating their message.

   Let me make sure I got this right, What I hear you saying is ...

2. Validate what you can by giving points when you can see why they may be feeling that way.

   I can see your point because I have been ...

3. Be emotionally responsive by joining with them in how they are feeling, comforting them, and seeking to understand more.

   I am sorry that you are been feeling this way. It is really important to me that I contribute to you feeling loved ...

4. Stay open to making changes and repair.

   Would it help if I…. What other things might help?

5. Come to agreement on an approach.

   So, we are in agreement then that we will ...

6. Have a monitoring process.

Principle 4: Manage the differences...with care and communication.

Proactive Strategies

1. **Identify your significant differences** by together taking the Couples Tendency Profile.

   - After taking the survey highlight any dimension where the difference is three points or more.

   - Consider looking back at your DISC styles to identify how the tendency difference may be reflective of a difference in your styles.

   - As an example, if you are three points or more different on the conflict dimension—that is, one person prefers avoiding conflicts, while the other prefers resolving conflicts, it may be reflective of the avoider being a high-S or high-C, while the resolver may be a high-D or high-I.

2. **Seek solutions that honor the key needs of both of you.** Use the consensus building strategies that you will learn in Principle 6, Addressing conflict.

- As an example, if your partner tends to be conflict-tolerant and you tend to be conflict-resolving, your experience might be that you typically want to know about an issue early so the two of you can quickly resolve it, while you partner typically doesn't want to bring up issues because they perceive them as being not such a big deal or not worth the effort.

- In seeking solutions, you may agree that when a conflict is apparent to either of you, you will seek to bring it up and the other partner will seek to always thank the partner for sharing, and then together you will decide a time to talk about it for further understanding, without the pressure of having to get to a solution right away.

3. **Establish creative approaches that work for the two of you in communicating and resolving differences.**

- Recognizing and communicating when a difference is showing up is a critical piece. Having a strategy to address a difference is also important, as you will see when I talk about intervention strategies.

4. **It's OK to grieve over the loss of tendencies that you wish your partner shared with you that you may have shared with previous partners.** But be open to seeing 1) how the differences can make your relationship different and unique, and 2) how the differences may be a strength for balancing you both and can help determine roles in the relationship.

Intervention Strategies

How do you recover if you or your partner has rejected rather than embraced a difference?

1. **Request a redo.**

   One of the fastest and easiest ways I teach couples to intervene during conflict is to say, "Stop. Can I have a redo and start over?" Emotional reactions are what typically happen automatically, so everyone is prone to a "slip" here and there. As soon as you or your partner are aware that you are not managing a difference well, activate this strategy!

2. **Practice assertive communication.**

   Slow things down by practicing the three main components of assertive communication:

   - Use I-statements.
     - For example, instead of saying, "You always need something from me," an appropriate I-statement might be, "I feel overwhelmed when you ask me to take care of your responsibilities."
     - I-statements reflect your thoughts and feelings to your partner. Using I-statements instead of You-statements helps disarm your partner and discourages them from reacting with defensive behaviors.

- Use feeling words.
  - Your partner is more likely to respond to you in a more loving way when you share a vulnerable feeling with them instead of blaming them for something and expecting them to respond in an empathic way.
  - I find that people often have difficulty identifying their deeper, more vulnerable feelings to their partner. Therefore, I recommend partners have a "feelings wheel" handy to help them identifying their deeper emotions. (You can download a feelings wheel by doing a search on this term using your favorite search engine.)
- Ask specifically for what you need.
  - A vague request can leave your partner feeling lost and not knowing what action to take. Therefore it is important that your request be specific as opposed to vague and general. This will help your partner understand how they can help you most effectively in the here and now.
  - For example, instead of saying, "I need to feel loved by you," say, "Will you come close and wrap your arms around me, so I feel your love?"

3. **Use reflective listening.**
   - Couples frequently make faulty assumptions about what their partner's words and/or actions mean.
   - When you and your partner are navigating through a difference, it can be very helpful to restate your partner's message often to let them know you understand them clearly before you move through the discussion. This strategy can drastically reduce unnecessary misunderstandings.

     Examples of how to start a reflective listening statement
     - *What I hear you saying is ...*
     - *Let me make sure I have this right ...*
     - *It sounds like what you are saying is .... Is that right?*
   - There may be times when your partner is not communicating with words. You can use reflective listening to reflect back the behavior you see versus what you hear. For example, you might say:
     - *I noticed you have been really quiet all day...*

4. **Seek solutions that respect the differences.**
   - In seeking solutions, you will want to use strategies we cover in Principle 6, Addressing conflict, for creating solutions to resolve conflict.
   - In seeking solutions, it is also important to avoid **A/B thinking.** A/B thinking occurs when one partner suggests A and the other suggests B, and the couple gets stuck arguing A versus B. Yet if they opened their discussion to seek other alternatives, they might find that there are other options (C, D, and E) that might be even better.

5. **Monitor the intervention for success.**
   - After you have implemented strategies to address a difference, be sure to check back in with each other to gain key learnings.
     - Was the strategy effective?
     - Is there more that needs to be done now to address this issue?
     - Is there a way we could have implemented the strategy to have made it even more effective?
     - Is there something we can do to help prevent the strategy from being needed in the future?

Principle 5: Avoid the fire starters...they can ignite a blaze.

Proactive Strategies

Use proactive strategies to prevent the fire before it starts. If you find **yourself** about to deliver a fire starter, try my **4-step Fire Prevention Strategy**.

1. Pause … count to five before you respond to allow time for the automatic negative reaction to pass.

2. Next, quickly remind yourself how much your partner means to you and how much you care about them.

3. Then consider the reaction you most desire from your partner (e.g., an apology, an expression of concern for you, a change in their behavior, etc.)

4. Finally, decide the words to use that would most likely evoke that reaction from your partner.

If you are unable to stay calm enough to use the fire prevention strategy, protect your relationship by calling a timeout and coming back to the table at an agreed upon time. Here's an example:

I want to take a timeout here. I'm starting to get irritated, and I know I won't be able to engage in a healthy conversation right now. This is important, so can we come back to this in a few hours once I have had chance to think about it more and calm down?

During that timeout period, keep reminding yourself that your partner is not you. They are different, not necessarily wrong. When you come back together focus on these four things:
- Practice gratitude.
- Talk openly about your needs and expectations.
- Practice active listening by listening to understand and provide feedback, instead of listening to react.
- Address your concerns in an assertive way with your partner.

Intervention Strategies

Use intervention strategies to extinguish the fire before it becomes a blaze. **If you find that you have delivered a fire starter to your partner**, immediately begin this 3-step extinguishing strategy.

Fire Extinguishing Strategy #1 (If you have delivered a fire starter)

1. Request a redo. *Stop. Can I have a redo and start over?*

2. Slow things down and apologize.

   I am frustrated and overreacted just now. I am sorry.

3. Practice assertive communication.
   - Use I-statements.
   - Use feeling words.
   - Ask specifically for what you need.

   It would be helpful to me if you would lower your voice and let me know that you are hearing me. What did you hear me say?

If your partner delivers a fire starter to you, rather than ignite the blaze, consider this 4-step extinguishing strategy.

Fire Extinguishing Strategy #2 (if your partner has delivered a fire starter)

1. Let your partner know the primary emotion you are feeling. (It's a good time to refer to your feeling wheel.) Let's take an example of your partner using the blaming fire starter.

   When you say it that way, I feel very blamed, and it makes it hard for me to hear you.

2. Ask your partner if they can state what they need using I-statements instead of a fire starter.

   It's pretty apparent that you are upset, and I am sorry for that. We've talked before about I-statements and that seems to work for us. I would appreciate it if you could use an I-statement to tell me how you are feeling or what you need from me.

3. Continue using the assertive communication and reflective listening strategies described in Principle 4, Managing the differences, to extinguish the fire starter.
   - Use I-statements.
   - Use feeling words.
   - Ask specifically for what you need.

4. Restate your partner's message often to let them know you understand them clearly before you move through the discussion.
   - What I hear you saying is …
   - Let me make sure I have this right …
   - It sounds like what you are saying is…. Is that right?

Once more, if you are unable to stay calm enough to use the fire extinguishing strategy, protect your relationship by calling a timeout and coming back to the table at an agreed upon time.

Principle 6: Address conflict...resolve disagreements.

Proactive Strategies

Preventing Level-1 Disagreements.

- Recall that level-1 disagreements are based on a lack of information. You can be proactive in preventing level-1 disagreements by being intentional about providing your partner all the information they may need to better understand the alternative you are proposing.
- If you find that you and your partner frequently have level-1 disagreements, do a debrief occasionally with each other. Ask, "What information could I have said before the disagreement started that would have prevented the disagreement from occurring?"
- You can use this information to inform how you present ideas to your partner in the future.

Preventing Level-2 Disagreements

- Level-2 disagreements are typically based on you and your partner having different values. You can help alleviate level-2 disagreements by being transparent, explicit, and proactive about sharing the values you hold that result in you preferring your alternative. Recall that you can get at values by identifying strengths. So, you might say, for example, "I want to do this because I value ..." and then speak about the strengths of your alternative.

Preventing Level-3 Disagreements

- Since level-3 disagreements are based on personality, past history, or other outside factors, you can be proactive in addressing level-3 disagreements by recognizing your own outside issues that may be impacting your view of the alternatives and being explicit and transparent about them.

In some cases, these proactive strategies can prevent the disagreement from occurring at all. In other cases, they can help resolve the disagreement more quickly and prevent it from becoming a conflict.

Intervention Strategies

Determining the Disagreement Level

So how do you determine if a disagreement is level-1, level-2 or level-3?

- First, determine if the disagreement is level 3. Recall the criteria. If any one of these exists, it is likely a level-3 disagreement.
  - Is there an unwillingness to share information?
  - Are the arguments irrational?
  - Is there a lack of commitment to finding a solution?

- If you can rule out level-3, then assume it is a level-1 disagreement and build a PAC and ask, "How would that work?" to ensure you both have the same information.

- If building a PAC doesn't resolve the issue, you can be confident that you are dealing with a level-2 disagreement and can use the level-2 resolution strategies.

Solving Level-1 Disagreements

If you find yourself disagreeing with something your partner says, and your sense is that it could be a source of conflict, slow down the conversation by doing what I call building a PAC.

Building a PAC

- **P**lay back what you believe you heard and confirm that you heard it correctly: *It sounds like you are saying ... is that right?*

- **A**gree with what you can agree with: *I certainly agree that ...*

- **C**hallenge by asking a question to address your concerns: *If we do this, how ...* or *How would that work?*

Solving Level-2 Disagreements

1. **Agree to try to resolve the disagreement using *The Porsha Principles* approach.**

2. **Identify what you agree on and confirm the source of the disagreement.**

3. **Confirm the alternatives and ask for others.**

4. **Identify the strengths of each alternative**. Together, define the strengths of each alternative over the other one. I recommend that you actually create a T-bar on paper and write down the strengths of each alternative so that you both can see them.

5. **Identify the weaknesses of each alternative**. After identifying the strengths of each alternative, together identify the weaknesses of each one. Note that if there are only two alternatives, this step may not be necessary, as the strengths of one alternative will likely be the weaknesses of the other.

6. **Check for agreement.**

7. **Isolate the key strengths.** Have each partner identify the one or two most important strengths of their alternative.

8. **Seek a merged alternative.** Ask, *Can we think of an alternative that combines these key strengths?*

Recognizing Level-3 Disagreements

Level-3 disagreements tend to exhibit at least one of the following telltale signs, and sometimes all three.

- **There is an unwillingness to share information.** If you partner is not willing to share their thinking or the reasons behind it, there may very likely be an outside factor causing the disagreement.

- **The arguments are irrational.** If you find that the reasons your partner gives for their disagreement don't appear to make sense, or if each time you address a reason they give a new reason pops up, there may be some outside factor causing the disagreement.
- **There is no commitment to finding a solution.** If you partner rejects every solution you come up with, without coming up with one themself, you may very well be dealing with a level-3 issue.

Solving Level-3 Disagreements

- **Empathize with the position.** If your partner is dealing with an outside factor that is impacting their interaction with you, it can be helpful to remind them how much you care about them and their happiness.

- **Use observation techniques and reflective listening**. State what you observe and reflect back what you think that might mean.

- **Ask for permission to dig deeper.**

- **Listen and affirm.** If your partner does share what the outside factor is, listen and affirm their concern, and seek resolution.

- **Let time pass if necessary.**

Principle 7: Repair the ruptures...they can ruin you.

Proactive Strategies

If you find yourself experiencing one of the early symptoms described above, consider the following actions.

1. Focus on Porsha Principles 2, 3 and 8 as daily practices in your relationship. These principles help keep you in the mindset of valuing your partner and the relationship.
   - Principle 2: Cultivate intimacy ... on deeper levels.
   - Principle 3: Lift your partner ... every day.
   - Principle 8: Profess, protect, and prioritize your relationship ... with your thoughts, words, and actions.

2. Hold weekly check-ins with your partner to avoid holding onto hurts until they become ruptures. In those weekly check-ins consider having each partner answer the following questions.
   - What went well this week in our relationship?
   - What were the events in this past week, if any, which felt like a small or big rupture?

3. To prevent a further rupture, and in addressing a rupture, it may be necessary to call a timeout. Take 30 minutes or more to identify what you need and why you were triggered. Be willing to reach for connection again with your partner at an agreed-upon time.

Intervention Strategies

When a rupture-causing event occurs, use the five-step intervention process discussed earlier and presented again below.

To Stabilize	To Strategize
The offending party should:	**Together they should:**
1. Address and fully understand the emotional impact their behavior had on their partner. 2. Express deep remorse, apologize, and take full ownership of their behavior without making excuses or trying to explain the behavior.	3. Isolate the likely root cause of the behavior. 4. Identify what could have been done to prevent it. 5. Identify where they are now and what will be done differently going forward.

Principle 8: Profess, protect, and prioritize the relationship...with your thoughts, words, and actions.

Proactive Strategies

Strategies to Profess Your Relationship

- Vocalize positive thoughts and feelings about your partner.
- Compliment your partner while speaking with others.
- Talk about your partner to others.
- Introduce your partner to your friends and family.
- Stand up for your partner.
- Support your partner's ideas and beliefs.

Strategies to Protect Your Relationship

- Set healthy boundaries in areas where needed.
- Be cautious about using words that might be misinterpreted by another person as indicating interest.
- Pay attention to your negative thoughts about your partner; remember, they influence your feelings and behaviors.
- Avoid such things as fantasizing about past relationships.
- Remove photos or mementos of previous relationships that would bring up memories of the past.
- Address your individual issues that can negatively impact a relationship—such as addictions, anxiety, depression, or other mental health issues. For example, if you suffer from depression, you may not want to do anything or be around other people. This can result in your partner feeling alone or unfulfilled.

- If you and your partner share a spiritual foundation, practice spirituality in your relationship by uplifting each other in prayer and looking for guidance from a higher power.
- Share experiences with your partner. When couples stop sharing experiences it can leave room for sharing those experiences with other people.
- Do things that your partner needs to feel loved but may not come naturally or are less enjoyable to you.
- Actively repair ruptures and proactively prevent them from happening.

Strategies to Prioritize Your Relationship

- Relax and unwind; take some time to focus on each other in a beautiful location.
- Create a bucket list of experiences you want to have together.
- Restate your acceptance of each other and your commitment to the relationship; this allows each of you to be who you are and to do the relationship work in a safe and supportive way.
- Hold a vow renewal in celebration of your love and dedication to one another.
- Take quarterly excursions to have time away alone with each other.
- Hold weekly date nights to maintain a regular romantic connection.
- Consider a couple's retreat to continue to build skills in sustaining healthy, positive interaction with one another.
- Find new fun things to do together to add variety and keep things exciting.
- Monitor how your partner is evolving by regularly checking in on changes to your partner's dreams, and to identify new interests and likes.

Intervention Strategies

1. **Don't be quiet.** When you feel a boundary has been violated, avoid being the silent martyr. Use assertive communication skills to bring up and address the issue, as described in Principle 4, Managing the differences:
   - Use I-statements.
   - Use feeling words.
   - Ask specifically for what you need.

2. **Be emotionally responsive.** Regardless of the degree of a rupture, if your partner is negatively impacted by an interaction with you or an action by you, you must be emotionally responsive by being accessible and emotionally comforting. Validate your partner's feelings, and make sure the rupture is repaired before you and your partner move on.

3. **Take responsibility.** Recall that some ruptures are scrapes—that is, simply caused by a difference, and no one is at fault. But if the rupture is a bruise or deep cut in which one of you is indeed at fault, part of the repair requires the offending partner to take responsibility as soon as possible for

their actions. Apologize, and continue to take the required steps to repair the rupture as described in Principle 7: Repair the ruptures.

4. **Be aware of differing interpretations.** Recognize that a bruise for one partner may, for the offending partner, be thought of as a minor scrape. For example, one person may feel that their partner is responsible for creating a bruise or deep cut and should apologize. However, the offending partner may feel it is a minor scrape and that their partner is being "too sensitive" or "overreacting." If the issue is just a matter of differences, it is important for both partners to recognize the difference and work out a solution for the future, versus creating a deeper rupture by arguing over who is at fault and who isn't.

About the Authors

Porsha Jones, LMFT

Porsha's ability to work so well with couples in crisis stems from her own personal history. After receiving her Bachelor of Arts degree in psychology from the University of California at Berkeley, she married her college sweetheart, who became a professional basketball player. Yet her life as a pro sports stay-at-home spouse abruptly ended when her husband suffered a sudden and fatal heart attack. Six months prior, her mother lost her battle with cancer at the age of 49. Left with a six-year-old son and no source of income or support, Porsha went back to school to pursue her passion in psychology and counseling. She graduated at the top of her class and received her Master of Family Therapy degree from Mercer University School of Medicine in Atlanta, and is currently a clinical member of the Georgia Association of Marriage and Family Therapy and the American Association of Marriage and Family Therapy.

> *Although I did not realize it at the time, it was from these tragedies that my journey as a marriage and family therapist actually began. My life's circumstances provided me both the ability to relate to others' pain, loss and trauma, and more importantly, the realization and confidence that one can heal, restore, and rise again.*

As a licensed marriage and family therapist, and a former pro sports wife, Porsha began working with professional athletes and their partners. She understood the specific lifestyle challenges athletes and their families face. She has been a featured therapist in *Professional Sports Lives Magazine* and the *Off the Field Player's Wives Association Newsletter*.

Her success with this elite audience quickly spread to elite levels in other professions, resulting in her working with CEOs, religious leaders, entertainers, and other celebrities. Though no longer offering couples counseling, she left private practice as one of the top marriage therapists in Atlanta.

Today, as founder of the Porsha Principles organization and co-author of *The Porsha Principals: A Practical Guide for Creating and Sustaining Your Lifelong Honeymoon*, Porsha continues her passion for helping couples create and sustain their lifelong honeymoon. Through her books, videos, workshops, and retreats, she has made her insights and strategies available to anyone who truly desires to do the work involved in creating highly satisfying and enjoyable relationships.

Michael Wilkinson, CMF

Michael is the founder and Managing Director of *Leadership Strategies, Inc. – The Facilitation Company,* the largest provider of professional facilitators and facilitation training in the U.S. He is considered an international leader in the facilitation industry.

- A Certified Master Facilitator, one of less than 50 in the world

- Founding board member of the International Institute for Facilitation

- Founder of the FindaFacilitator database, with over 600 facilitators under contract

- Author of *The Secrets of Facilitation, The Secrets to Masterful Meetings, The Executive Guide to Facilitating Strategy, Buying Styles* and *CLICK: The Virtual Meetings Book*

- Named to the International Facilitation Hall of Fame in 2016

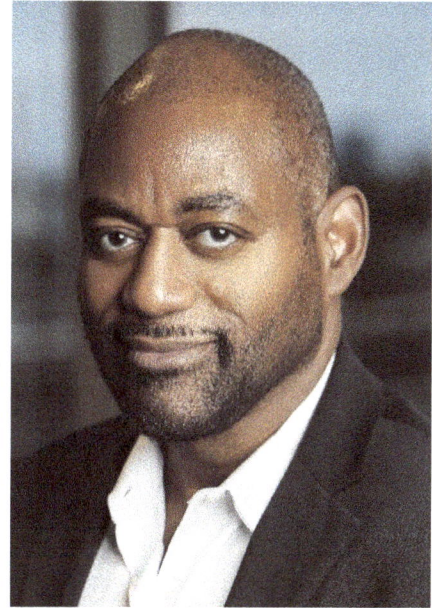

Michael is a much sought-after facilitator, trainer, and speaker, both in the U.S. and around the globe. He has completed international assignments in Bangkok, Beijing, Brisbane, Geneva, Glasgow, Hamburg, Helsinki, Hong Kong, Istanbul, Jamaica, London, Melbourne, Milan, Moscow, the Netherlands, Oxford, Saint Petersburg, Saudi Arabia, Singapore, Stockholm, Sydney, Trinidad, Vienna, Warsaw, and Wellington. Past participants have commented that his dynamic presentation style, combined with his unique insights, make for intense, power-packed sessions.

> *I was blessed by Our Creator with a passion to help others and the ability to package ideas into practical, repeatable strategies. It didn't take long for Porsha and me to see how our strengths were a wonderful gift to each other and potentially to the world.*

Prior to *Leadership Strategies,* Michael spent six years with ADP and eight years in the information technology practice of Ernst & Young's Management Consulting Group.

As Chief Operating Officer of the Porsha Principles organization, Michael oversees the team of employees and contractors that help the organization thrive. He is a spiritual teacher and a high honors graduate from Dartmouth College, has two adult daughters, and resides in Atlanta with Porsha, the woman he is creating and sustaining his lifelong honeymoon with.

www.ingramcontent.com/pod-product-compliance
Lightning Source LLC
Chambersburg PA
CBHW081435270326
41932CB00019B/3212

* 9 7 8 0 9 7 2 2 4 5 8 9 0 *